THE WORLD CHRISTIAN

Written and Edited by
Robin Thomson

Contributors
Steve Chalke, Stanley Davies
Dick Dowsett, Ram Gidoomal
Yemi Ladipo, Chris Sugden

Consultant
Jonathan Ingleby

Design
Simon Jenkins
& Paul Clowney

LYNX

ST JOHN'S
EXTENSION
STUDIES

Published by **Lynx Communications**
Peter's Way, Sandy Lane West,
Oxford, OX4 5HG
in association with St John's Extension Studies,
Bramcote, Nottingham NG9 3DS
ISBN 0 7459 2540 5

© St John's Extension Studies 1991

**Printed in Great Britain by
Antony Rowe Ltd, Chippenham, Wiltshire**

Acknowledgments

We gratefully acknowledge the co-operation of the Christmas Cracker Trust in the preparation of this workbook, in particular towards the provision of the graphic design. This indicates their commitment to the cause of world mission.

We also acknowledge permission to use copyright material from the following:

The World Christian Handbook, edited by David Barrett, 1982, by permission of Oxford University Press.

The Bible and the Flag, Brian Stanley, Apollos, Leicester, 1990.

Student Training in Mission, a training manual published by InterVarsity Christian Fellowship, Madison, USA.

Jesus and the World Religions, Ajith Fernando, STL/MARC, 1988.

There's a Big World Out There, Val and Dan Connolly, Portsmouth.

CONTENTS

How to Use this Book

HOW TO USE THIS BOOK

This is a workbook. That doesn't mean that you won't enjoy it! On the contrary, we are sure that you will find it stimulating, exciting, even fun (sometimes!).

You are free to use it like any other book—pick it up whenever you want, turn to the pages you like, and skip the others. You will still get a lot from it. But you will get even more if you understand how it has been planned for you to use.

Each unit contains two parts:

■ **Part A** introduces the topic and contains material for you to work through on your own. At the end is a section for *group* discussion and activity.

■ **Part B** is called 'Going Further'. It gives suggestions for further study and reading, projects and assignments.

Three options

The material in the book is intended to be used in at least three ways...

■ group discussion and activity

■ individual study

■ individual study for credit, with the help of a tutor from St John's Extension Studies

You can combine these in various ways. For example, you might be part of a group and then decide later to do the individual study on your own or with a tutor. Or you could study it yourself and later share it with a group in your church or fellowship. Or...

Let's look at these three options in turn.

Group study

Look for the group activity page at the end of Part A in each unit.

All the group members should work through Part A before the meeting. That will make your group discussion and activity much more enjoyable. Even a brief reading will make all the difference. If your group does not have a regular leader, choose one person beforehand to lead the session.

The leader will need to work through the whole of Part A carefully and choose which questions and activities the group is going to discuss. *Most groups will not have time to discuss everything, so it is important to make your own choice.*

Leading a group discussion requires certain skills, of course—choosing the right questions, drawing people out and avoiding talking too much yourself! But the leader does not need any specialist knowledge beyond what is in the book.

Individual study

Work through Part A of each section and then spend as much time as you wish on Part B. This usually contains readings, suggestions for further study and optional projects or assignments.

Studying with a tutor

This book is the introductory module to the study programme *Culture to Culture* (see Unit 8 for further information about that). If you want to do the longer course, then you are required to work through all the material in this book, including the assignments.

You will need to do the following...

1 Register your name with St John's Extension Studies. (Use the registration form at the end of the book.) You will be assigned a correspondence tutor.

2 Work through the whole book and do the required assignments.

3 Send them to your tutor for assessment. On satisfactory completion you will receive a certificate and will be eligible to continue with the longer course, if you wish.

If you have any questions at any time, you will be able to contact your tutor by letter or phone. You will get full details when your tutor's name is sent to you.

There will be a charge for having this tutorial help. This is payable at the time of registration. See the form at the end of the book.

You can decide to register for credit at any time. For example, you may have used this book with a group or in individual study and then later decide that you want to get credit. All you have to do is register and then, after you have been assigned a tutor, complete the required assignments. It will take much less time, because you will already be familiar with the material.

Making responses

When you look at the material in either part, you will find that it often asks you questions, suggests an activity, or invites a response. You will learn best if you respond, preferably in writing, in the spaces provided. Don't be hesitant to write in the book—that's what it's for! Of course if you prefer, you can write your responses on a separate paper or in a notebook.

You may find the wide margins useful to write in, if the spaces aren't big enough.

If you are in a group you will discuss your answers (whether written or not). But even if you are on your own you will be able to enter into discussion with the contents of this book and the questions it raises in your mind.

You will find that stimulating and you will learn much more—because most of the answers will be ones that you have thought through for yourself.

As you respond to the book's questions, you will sometimes find that the text then gives its own response, which you can compare with yours. This helps you to confirm your response, or think about alternative answers.

CULTURE
to CULTURE

THE WORLD CHRISTIAN

Unit 1

ONE WORLD GOD'S WORLD

CONTENTS

PURPOSE

PART A The purpose of this unit is to help you to realise the spread, diversity and impact of the Christian church around the world today. As a result, you will find out information about the church in a particular region of the world and strengthen your existing links with Christians and churches from other regions and cultures.

PART B You will present your information in a form suitable for a church group.

All statistics in this unit are taken from *The World Christian Encyclopaedia*, edited by David Barrett, by permission of Oxford University Press, 1982. Some have been further updated from *Our Globe and How to Reach It*, by David Barrett and Todd Johnson, AD2000 Series, New Hope, 1990.

THE GLOBAL VILLAGE?

NORTH & SOUTH

EAST & WEST

BLACK & WHITE

**YOUNG AND OLD
RICH AND POOR
URBAN AND RURAL
HOT AND COLD
WET AND DRY**

One world: the global village?

It really is. Satellites, computers, faxes, chips with everything. Today it's the World Cup. Tomorrow it's Wimbledon or cricket or the Olympics. The winning goal will be seen all round the world at once.

But not only goals. The crowds in Manila, Peking, Leipzig or Prague… We all saw them and that's what made the difference. We watched with horror as the tanks rolled into Tiananmen Square; with amazement and delight as they didn't come to Eastern Europe. We can see riots and demonstrations, famine victims, flood victims, earthquake victims, politicians, hostages, even executions. It excites us. Sometimes it chills us. Or just bores us as we hop to the next channel.

3-2-1

Not long ago the world was neatly divided into three worlds. There was 'us' and two kinds of 'them' – whichever direction you were looking from. That's changing rapidly. The Third World doesn't like to be called that. and in any case it's exceedingly diverse. And the Second World – of Communist countries – is rapidly breaking up. Perhaps we'll end up with just two worlds – the 'haves' and the 'have nots'. Or perhaps we'll find new ways to divide ourselves up.

A dying world?

Hotter summers, failure of rainfall, droughts, storms, toxic waste, Chernobyl, Three Mile Island…

Will we die of thirst or will we poison ourselves first? It's the question nobody can answer and not many like to ask or think about.

God's world

We wonder. The Bible says that God is in control but it isn't always easy to see. Of course, many disasters can be blamed on our human selfishness and stupidity – but not all.

Some people are trying to use religious beliefs to unite people – over the environment, for example. There is a growing conviction among many that we need a 'world religion', a blend of the best in all religious traditions.

Others find that religion only

seems to divide. Catholics and Protestants kill each other just because they are Catholic or Protestant. So do Hindus and Muslims, Jews and Arabs, Buddhists and Hindus, Christians and Muslims, high-caste and low-caste…

God's people in God's world

Here's something that is less often talked about. About 33% of the world call themselves Christian. They claim in some way to be God's people (though quite a lot of them hardly stop to think about that, or even to think about God). That's about 1700 million people. Of them about 1000 million are active church members. They live in 'every inhabited country on earth' (Barrett, p.1).

This is what Archbishop William Temple called 'The great new fact of our era… a Christian fellowship which now extends into almost every nation' (he was speaking about 50 years ago).

Stop and think

Look at the box below. What strikes you about these figures? Are there any surprises?

Which religions do you think are the most 'missionary'?

- Atheism
- Christianity
- Hinduism
- Islam

HOW MUCH DO YOU KNOW?

How much do you know about world Christianity? Before looking at the rest of this unit, try these questions:

1. What is the language of the largest number of Christians?
- English
- French
- Spanish
- Korean

2. Which languages have more than 10 million Christian speakers?
- Russian
- Quechua
- Tagalog
- Korean
- Arabic

4. Which countries have the largest number of Protestant missionaries from abroad?
- Brazil
- Japan
- India
- Papua New Guinea
- USA

3. How many languages is the Bible translated into?
- 2,500
- 1048
- 318

5. How many Christian denominations are there in the world?
- 260
- 6,000
- 22,000

6. What is the distribution of Christians between 'South' and 'North' today. (The 'North' is the industrialised, wealthier countries of the world — from both hemispheres. The 'South' is the poorer, less developed countries.)
- North 83% / South 17%
- 51% / 49%
- 29% / 71%

7. What is the proportion between 'white' and 'non-white' Christians in the world today?
- 38:62
- 81:19
- 48:52

Answers on page 6 ➡

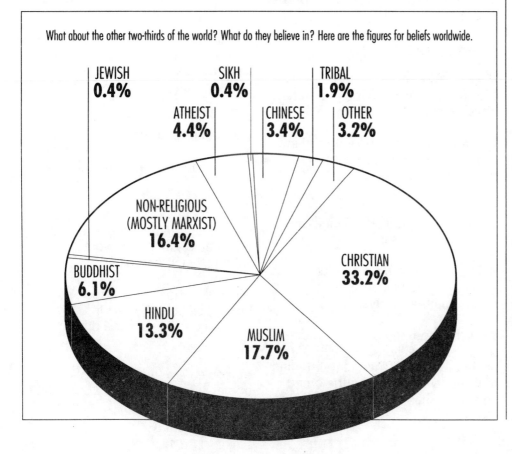

What about the other two-thirds of the world? What do they believe in? Here are the figures for beliefs worldwide.

JEWISH **0.4%** SIKH **0.4%** TRIBAL **1.9%**

ATHEIST **4.4%** CHINESE **3.4%** OTHER **3.2%**

NON-RELIGIOUS (MOSTLY MARXIST) **16.4%**

BUDDHIST **6.1%**

HINDU **13.3%**

MUSLIM **17.7%**

CHRISTIAN **33.2%**

GOD'S DIVERSE PEOPLE

A worldwide family

The church exists around the world, and it's astonishingly diverse. It reads the Bible in 318 languages, the New Testament in 1048 languages, and parts of the Bible in 2,500 languages.

The church is divided into three large families: Catholic, Protestant, Orthodox – and many groups or denominations within these broader families.

> **"For the first time there is in the world a universal religion... the Christian religion."** Stephen Neill

Over the last 60 years or so a whole new 'family' has emerged, of 'Non-White Indigenous' churches – churches that have been started and developed quite independently of the three historic families.

From choirboys to drive-ins...

The church worships God in different ways. Think of...

■ a cathedral evensong with organ, choirboys, robed processions, quiet dignified chants.

■ a football stadium of people singing, listening to an evangelist or waving their arms in the air.

■ a house in China packed full of people, overflowing into all the rooms and the courtyards.

■ several thousand people in India sitting for three hours on the floor under a great thatched tent, listening to three sermons, taking the bread and wine, sharing a meal together at the end.

■ three or four men and women huddled together in a room in Afghanistan or Saudi Arabia. They don't know each other's surnames. They just 'happened' to come to the house that afternoon. If others find out they would be killed.

■ thousands and thousands of 'ordinary' congregations meeting in church buildings of stone, brick, wood, canvas, cement, glass.

■ people sitting, standing or kneeling all through the service.

■ people singing *Songs of Fellowship* with guitars. Others singing hymns and choruses that are recognisably Western, though in different languages. Others with tunes and rhythms that are all their own.

■ people clapping, dancing, in African independent churches.

■ churches with Gothic architecture in Africa or India. Others with all kinds of experiments in buildings, or no building at all.

■ those in Orthodox churches who wear robes and swing censers of incense. Meanwhile in Papua New Guinea they're wearing feathers and paint.

■ services where children are free to crawl around, mothers are feeding their babies, men and women are sitting strictly segregated.

■ people who come on foot, by bicycle, by boat, by car! In California they stay in the car for a drive-in service.

■ people who 'go to church' at home, in front of their TV or by the radio.

THE BIBLE HAS BEEN TRANSLATED INTO

318

LANGUAGES

TRENDS IN THE WORLD CHURCH

North and South

By the year 2000, Christians in the 'south' will have overtaken 'northern' Christians in numbers.

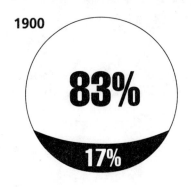

1900

83%

17%

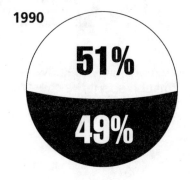

1990

51%

49%

White and non-white

AD 500	
38%	62%
AD 1000	
61%	39%
AD 1900	
81%	19%
AD 1985	
47%	53%
AD 2000?	

THE SEVEN FAMILIES

The TOP SEVEN Families (or major church groupings) are as follows...

1	Roman Catholic	872 million	58.7%
2	Protestant (excluding Anglican)	278 million	18.7%
3	Orthodox	170 million	11.5%
4	Indigenous	95 million	6.4%
5	Anglican	51 million	3.4%
6	Sects (unorthodox)	16 million	1.1%
7	Catholic (non-Roman)	3.6 million	0.2%

REFLECTION & QUESTIONS

Well, how much did you know? Were there any surprises as you looked at all the information about the church around the world? Note here anything which particularly struck you:

You may be wondering about the figures… Are there really that many Christians in the world? Or perhaps you thought there were more.

We must point out that the figures in the *World Christian Encyclopaedia* include *everybody* who is in some way identified with some branch of the Christian church. So they cover a very broad spectrum.

But of course, the same is true for the figures of Hindus or Muslims or Marxists or any other faith. They all include 'nominal' adherents as well as the committed members.

Do figures matter at all? That's something that you could discuss – in your group if you are doing this with a group, or with your friends. For example, is a group's influence necessarily in proportion to its numerical size? Write your thoughts here:

Which are the most 'missionary' religions today? It's impossible to give a statistical answer. But while atheism is on the decline, all three of the others mentioned in the 'Stop and think' section on page 3 actively propagate their faith and claim to be universal. (Does that surprise you about Hinduism? But it's true.) Our world is a marketplace of ideas, beliefs and values, claiming to be true, competing for our hearts and minds. Any comments about that?

One further comment about numbers. David Barrett describes two pitfalls in looking at large tables of numbers. One is triumphalism: 'Spectacular growth or numerical success do not in themselves spell spiritual depth or significant progress. We need to disavow… triumphalism, and to replace it by service in the name of Christ'.

The other pitfall is to treat all these numbers as impersonal and forget that they represent individuals, all of whom are important. We are all part of these figures, so they can't be completely impersonal!

ANSWERS TO THE QUIZ

(on page 3)

1. Spanish (207 million) Though English is actually spoken by a far larger number of Christians as a second language

2. All of them

3. Complete Bibles: 318; New Testaments: 1,048; portions of the Bible: 2,500

4. Brazil. All the countries listed have over 2,000 Protestant missionaries from abroad. The USA has over 5,000 Christian workers from abroad, though most would not be 'missionaries' in the strict sense.

5. 22,000. Of these 6,000 are numerically significant. There are about 260 new denominations each year.

6. North 51%; South 49%. In 1900 the proportion was 83:17

7. 48:52. It was 81:19 in 1900

Some churches are very 'Westernised'. Others are 'indigenous'. What makes the difference? Is it important? Write your comments here:

Which styles of worship have you encountered, apart from your own regular way of worship? For example 'liturgical' (with a fixed order of service) or 'free' (hymns etc) or 'very free' (choruses, clapping, lots of participation) or…?

What has surprised you about other styles of worship that you have encountered? What has impressed you? What features would you like to include in your own worship?

The church's impact

We've seen the church's amazing diversity. We've thought a bit about numbers (more of them later). But what impact do Christians actually have on the world around them? Because they aren't meant to stay only in church.

Stop and think

What influence does the church in your area have on society? Can you think of examples?

IMPACT ON SOCIETY

Christian impact

You don't find Christians only in church, of course. You find them at their daily work – working hard and honestly (for the most part).

Feeding the hungry; starting new health programmes; pioneering education, especially for women and children; looking after the handicapped and neglected; seeking out the dying to give them dignity in death, whether beggars in Calcutta streets or AIDS patients in high rise apartments.

Demonstrating in the streets; holding prayer vigils; leading processions; pioneering trade unions; campaigning against slavery, tobacco, alcohol, nuclear arms. Campaigning for women's emancipation, improved prison conditions, better nursing care. Going to prison for their faith.

The rough and the smooth

In some places it's costly to be a Christian – it could cost you your life, freedom, family membership, ostracism by friends, small humiliations, jeering and teasing. It could mean standing apart from your associates, or from common practices and customs.

In other places, it's easy, even fashionable. You are going along with the opinion of leaders or people in government, education, the media. So much so that you can be a nominal Christian without thinking about it too much.

Failures

Sometimes Christians fail as well. Sometimes they have not got involved in standing for justice and caring for the needy. They've kept out of these struggles from conviction – or from cowardice or apathy. They've cared for their own community or class. They've identified with colonialism or economic exploitation.

They've failed to think and to question. They've been negative and old fashioned, alienated from young people and thinkers. They've cut themselves off from culture, or identified too closely with it. They've exported cultural values that had no relevance for the Gospel.

They've seen churches close and congregations shrink or disappear, as well as those that have expanded. They have allowed the scandal of division to take place – and to increase in our day – despite the fact that our faith is based on Jesus' command to 'love one another... as I have loved you'.

EVERY YEAR THERE ARE

260

NEW DENOMINATIONS

DENOMINATIONS

There are more than 22,000 denominations in the world today. Five new denominations are started *every week* (totalling about 260 a year).

Out of these 22,000 denominations, about 6,000 are numerically significant. The rest are splinter groups – mostly caused by clashes over personality or property, power and prestige.

David Barrett comments: 'In many countries this produces serious overlapping, competition, rivalries, clashes, violence and even lawsuits and protracted litigation.' The confusion and even scandal that this vast fragmentation generates in the minds of non-Christians can be imagined.

... and lead us not into denomination, but deliver ...

Stop and think

Is the church growing or declining today? Write your observations here:

Answering this question partly depends what we mean by 'growth' and 'decline'. Do we think in numbers only, or are there other ways of measuring growth and decline? Write here the different factors you would include.

1.

2.

3.

4.

5.

What is happening in the different churches in your area? Growth, decline, or what? You could try listing the local churches and finding out from them how they see their situation.

Do you think the same is true in other parts of the world? Give reasons for your answer!

Failure

Christians fail, too. Can you think of ways in which they have failed?

■ In the past?

■ In your area, in the present?

■ In other parts of the world that you know of?

THE FAST–SLOW QUIZ

Where do you think the church is growing fastest? Put against each country: F (fast growth) S (slow growth) or D (decline or no growth).

■ Australia

■ Britain

■ Finland

■ Greece

■ Indonesia

■ Italy

■ Kenya

■ Korea

■ Libya

■ Sudan

■ Sweden

■ USA

Answers on page 11 ➡

Very rapid church growth (over 4% per year) is taking place in **28** countries

Rapid church growth (3%–4% p.a) is taking place in **42** countries

Moderate church growth (1–3% p.a) is taking place in **77** countries

Little or no church growth (0–1% p.a) is taking place in **48** countries

GROWTH AND DECLINE

From rapid growth to catastrophe

That is a picture of the church around the world. David Barrett sums it up by saying: 'In vast areas of the world, the church of Jesus Christ is growing rapidly. In many other areas it is declining gradually, and in a few other areas it is declining catastrophically.'

Just look at the facts...

Statistics of hope and challenge

David Barrett's figures chart the growth and decline of the modern church: 'On the one hand Christianity has experienced massive gains across the Third World throughout the 20th century.' In real terms this means...

■ 65 new congregations a day around the world
■ In Africa 16,400 new Christians a day.
■ In E. Asia 1,000 new Christians a day
■ In South Asia 3,000 new Christians a day

David Barrett concludes that 'a major reason for this expansion... is the attracting power of the Christian Gospel of justice and the love of God for the poor and oppressed'

However, there is a dark side to the picture as well: 'But on the other hand, Christianity has experienced massive losses in the Western and Communist worlds over the last 60 years. In the Soviet Union Christians have fallen from 83.6% in 1900 to 36.1% today.' In Europe and North America, a similar decline means a loss of 7,600 people *every day*.

Evangelism

It is hard to quantify evangelism. At what point have people been evangelised? How do we know that people have heard and understood the message of Christ? How do we assess people's response or the state of their hearts and consciences? Only God knows.

But however we measure, it is safe to say that there are over 1,500 million 'unevangelised persons unaware of Christianity, Christ and the Gospel' (Barrett p.19) That is about one third of the world, almost the same as the number of Christians. That is quite apart from the other one third of the world who may have heard and perhaps understood, and the many nominal Christians...

People groups

It is sometimes helpful to think, not only of individuals, but of 'people groups', that is, significantly large

WHICH PART OF THE WORLD?

Where do you think this place is? It is an area of 3 miles by 4 miles, in which 220,000 people live. Almost half the population is non-European: West Indians, Indians, Pakistanis, Bangladeshis, Chinese, Africans etc. It is a unique situation in Europe, if not the whole world, to have so many ethnic groups in the one small area. It is an area in which the church strength is approx. 1,500 or 0.5% of the population – a church declining and dying. The area is the London Borough of Newham.

ethnic or sociological groups of individuals who perceive themselves to have a common affinity for each other. This would mean that the Gospel could spread through such a group without having to cross further cultural barriers.

There are many thousands of such 'people groups' in the world, classified in different ways. Some have over 1 million members (megapeoples) while others have only a few hundred.

It is estimated that 12,000 people groups today are 'unreached peoples'. That is, they have no indigenous community of believing Christians with adequate numbers and resources to evangelise them. Several hundred of them have less than 0.1% church members (one in 1,000).

Such groups are sometimes referred to as 'hidden peoples', because the gospel is effectively hidden from them and they are 'out of sight' of Christian attention.

The number of the unevangelised is in fact greater today than at any time in history (even though the number of Christians is also greater).

There is, however, some evidence that the impact and influence of Christianity is still increasing, despite the obstacles.

> **"In vast areas of the world, the church of Jesus Christ is growing rapidly. In many other areas it is declining gradually, and in a few other areas it is declining catastrophically."** David Barrett

Christianity in the 20th century

David Barrett sums up his facts and figures in the following way: 'The status of Christianity at this point in history presents a striking paradox. On the one hand, the 20th century has seen a marked decline in the number of committed Christians in proportion to the world. But on the other hand, the impact and influence of those adherents on the world scene has expanded phenomenally. In Jesus' day, the rapid growth of a mustard seed startled His followers; in the same way today, the vast expansion of the influence of the Kingdom of God exceeds all the expectation of earlier generations of Christians.' (Barrett p.19)

> **All thought of a post-Christian world is "glib... naive and hasty."** K.S. Latourette

ANSWERS TO THE QUIZ
(on page 9)

Fast growth: Korea, Kenya, Sudan, Indonesia

Slow growth: Australia, Greece, USA, Sweden

Decline or no growth overall: Britain, Finland, Italy, Libya

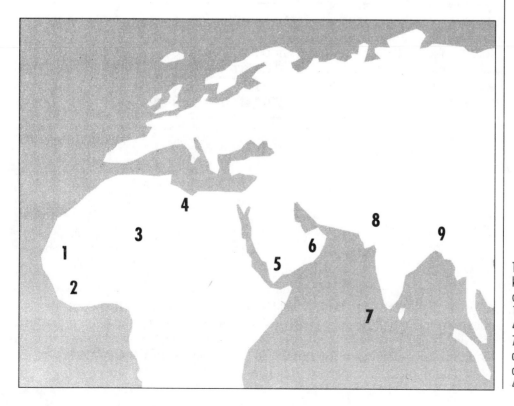

THE BOTTOM NINE

The location of the 'unevangelised' is known. The nine least evangelised countries in the world are:
1. Mauritania, 2. Guinea, 3. Sahara, 4. Libya, 5. North Yemen, 6. Oman, 7. Maldive Islands, 8. Afghanistan and 9. Bhutan. The total population of these areas in 1980 was just over 41 million.

REFLECTION

What strikes you most as you think of the church's growth or decline around the world? Did any of the information surprise you? If so, what?

Can we learn from the experience of Christians in other parts of the world? In what ways? Write down some practical suggestions:

Have we really grasped the fact of the spread, diversity and impact of the church around the world?
That's a fact to thank God for. It's also a challenge for us – to think how best we can link ourselves with the world church, to receive and learn as well as to give and share. Look at paragraphs A and B on the opposite page. If you are studying on your own, write down your answers to the questions here.

As you conclude this study, you will have plenty to think about and lots of questions. How did we get to this position today? Why did the church grow and decline? Who helped it to spread? Why have churches in other countries inherited the problems, divisions and cultural patterns of Western churches? We will look at these questions in unit 2.

GROUP ACTIVITIES

Activities

A. One third of the world call themselves Christian. What about the others? If 10 people represented the earth's population, their beliefs would divide up as shown on the right.

Divide your group into these proportions. (If there are 10 of you, it will be easier!) What do you think about these figures? Are there any surprises?

How do you feel about the proportion of Christians? Do we sometimes live and act as though we were a much smaller minority, worldwide? Discuss the question about numbers on page 6, if you have time.

B. What strikes you most as you think of the diversity of the church around the world (styles of worship, church forms, denominations, different emphases)? Do you feel comfortable about it – or do you wish that other Christians were 'more like us'? Do you wish that we were all more united?

C. If you have access to a video this would be a good point to watch it. Two that are recommended: **Jesus Commands us to Go** (SIM International), **Across Cultures** (Interserve). See the Introduction for details.

Discuss what you learn about the church in other parts of the world (not just what missionaries from your place are doing).

D. Do you have any connections with Christians in other parts of the world? This might be through Christians from other cultures in your locality. Or it could be through links with individuals, churches or groups in other areas. Share the information you have in your group. What have you learned or gained from your connections? What similarities or differences have you found?

E. How could you find out more, or turn your existing links into even more effective partnership? Discuss your ideas. These might include...

■ Contacting overseas students/visitors in your locality.
■ Finding out about churches with a different cultural background.
■ Corresponding with another church, or even getting 'twinned' with them.
■ Inviting Christians from other areas to give their comments on your church life.

F. **Project** Find out as much as you can about the church in another part of the world. See Part B for suggestions (page 14).
Alternatively, you could monitor the media for a week. Look out for any reference to Christians in the stories, news headlines, etc. Find out their situation in the world's most newsworthy regions.

In conclusion...

Close your session with a brief time of prayer:

■ Thank God for His church around the world.

■ Thank God for the links you already have and all that you have gained.

■ Ask God to help you to develop more effective links.

■ Pray for Christians in other parts of the world known to you.

■ Pray for Christians (unknown to you) in places of the world that are in the news this week.

If a group of 10 people represented the earth's population, then roughly...

3 of them would be Christians...

2 of them would be Muslims...

1.5 of them would be non-religious (including Marxists)...

a further 1.5 would be Hindu...

1 would be Buddhist or follow a Chinese faith...

and the final 1 would represent Atheists, Tribal Religionists, Jews, Sikhs and others.

For the exact proportions, see the chart on page 3.

GOING FURTHER

Getting to know the family

We are part of a worldwide family. So it is important for us to know as much as we can about the family members. On the other hand, it is probably impossible for us to know about all of them in depth (unless we happen to be editing the *World Christian Encyclopaedia*!)

So try to find out something more about the church in one region of the world. If you already know quite a bit about some region (other than your own) use this opportunity to find out about another.

Reading material

Two excellent reference books for finding out more about the worldwide church are: *The Quiet Revolution* (Lion Publishing), and *Ripening Harvest: Gathering Storm* by Maurice Sinclair.

See the Introduction for further details of these books. Both give valuable surveys of the situation of the church in six continental regions.

Use the books in the following way...

1. Choose one region and read the survey from either book (the page numbers are listed on the left).

2. Supplement your reading with any other information you can get (from the media, library, church or missionary magazine, etc.). *Operation World* is also a very valuable resource, giving great detail.

3. Make a brief summary of your information. Put it in a form that you can present to others – for example your Youth Fellowship, church or other group.

This could be in the form of an article for the church magazine or material for an existing programme for the group, or a Sunday evening Service, prayer meeting etc.

If you are able to use it, note down your reflections on the experience.

For registered students

This summary will be one of the assignments to be sent to your tutor. It should be 600-800 words in length (apart from any instructions about how it is to be presented if it is material for group discussion etc.).

You should highlight the following:

■ How the church in that region is the same as the church in your area.

■ How it is different from the church in your area.

■ Lessons that we can learn from the church in that region.

Send your summary in now so that your tutor can be looking at it while you move on to unit 2.

CONTINENT BY CONTINENT

The following page numbers refer to the books *The Quiet Revolution* (Lion Publishing), and *Ripening Harvest: Gathering Storm* by Maurice Sinclair.

Africa: Lion pp135–155, Sinclair pp101–110

Asia: Lion pp156–181, Sinclair pp111–120

Pacific: Lion pp182–195, Sinclair pp134–137

Europe: Lion pp196–217, Sinclair pp121–133

Latin America: Lion pp218–243, Sinclair pp146–155

North America: Lion pp244–267, Sinclair pp138–145

Summary: Sinclair pp156–158

POSTSCRIPT: 'THIRD WORLD'

It has been fashionable for some years to talk about the 'Third World' in connection with missionary work. It sounds much more modern than the old 'mission field' which our parents referred to.

But the 'Third World' is a slippery term. There are several explanations of its origin and what it means. Some link it with poverty and economic disparities. For others it is political: parallel to the Non-Aligned Movement, not part of the capitalist or communist blocs.

Some link the 'Third World' with the former colonies, politically independent but now even more dependent economically on rich countries and multinational corporations. For others the 'Third World' is the poor and oppressed in *every* part of the world.

The term 'Third World' does reflect some economic, social and political realities. However, some say that it has lost its usefulness. The 'Third World' nations are so diverse that it is totally misleading to talk of them as though they were a unity.

With the break up of the 'Second World' – the communist bloc – it is time to re-evaluate these terms in any case. 'Cold war certainties' have disappeared.

Third World church?

However, our purpose here is more specific. Whatever we think of the 'Third World', is this the right term to use when we think of the *church* around the world? When we do so we tend to see 'Third World churches' as an abstraction, bound together by their common situation.

We go to 'serve in the Third World' (two or three years, enough to salve the conscience) or we exploit our 'Third World' identity to raise money from rich Christians in the West.

We evoke the old connotations of paternalism and dependence, 'non-alignment' in response to 'missionary domination'. Or we create a romantic picture of 'growth in Third World churches' – usually overflowing with 'national' Christians. ('Nationals' and 'national churches' are always 'Third

World'; we don't talk about them in Europe or Australia).

These stereotypes do not correspond to reality. They blur the rich diversity of the church around the world.

Signs of life

What are the actual characteristics of churches around the world? Let us look at some of the usual indicators of a church's vitality. Generalisations are dangerous, but here are some. They are partial and impressionistic.

■ **Spiritual vitality** A vague term but we know what it means! Wherever you look, you find great variety, the heights and depths. Renewals and revivals alongside nominal Christianity. No part of the world has a monopoly on spiritual growth or decline. However, it is interesting that the the East Africans made the greatest impact in this aspect at the Lausanne Congress on World Evangelisation in 1974.

■ **Evangelism** It is impossible to generalise. Clearly the countries where the church is growing fastest are not in the west. That does not mean that methods used in one place can always be transferred. But it is safe to say that western Christians can learn about evangelism from other churches.

■ **Suffering and pressure** The church in the West has everything to learn from those who suffer under atheist regimes, intolerant dictatorships or religious fanaticism. There are as many martyrs today as at any period (about 250,000 a year, according to some estimates).

■ **Cross-cultural mission** the majority of missionaries have been from the West in the last two to three centuries. But that is rapidly changing, as we shall see in Unit 2.

■ **Availability of the Bible** English-speaking Christians have plenty of translations (too many?), while others do not have any. And some who have the Bible cannot use it freely because of

Shiva Naipaul describes the "illusion of the Third World... a form of bloodless universality that robs other individuals and societies of their particularity... People only look alike when you can't be bothered to look at them closely... The exemplary Third World denizen... lives a hand-to-mouth existence, he is indifferent to the power struggle of the mighty ones and he is dark-skinned."
An Unfinished Journey

WAYS OF SEEING THE WORLD

Some people talk about the Two Thirds World. That's better, because it reflects the numerical balance, and also gets away from 'Third World' connotations. But it still creates a dichotomy which is increasingly irrelevant today.

A few years ago we used to talk about 'older' and 'younger' churches. Then it became 'national' churches (whatever that means). But Stephen Neill once pointed out that there are really just two kinds of churches – static churches and dynamic churches. And both kinds are found all over the world.

Another way to look at the world is being projected by David Barrett and associates (*Our Globe and How to Reach it*):
- **World A** The unevangelised – those who have never heard the gospel.
- **World B** Those who have heard but have not yet responded to Christ.
- **World C** Christians, of all kinds. Worlds A and B comprise 66% of our world (another 'Two Thirds World'?) They are found in every part of it. They should be our priority. But 95% of our attention and resources are given to World C.

political or religious pressures.

■ **Christian literature** Here again, English readers suffer from a glut – and so much of it third or fourth rate. Many other languages are starved by comparison. But the real tragedy is that much Christian publishing is simply aimed at the Christian market.
Contrast *Breakthrough* or *Magalla*, Christian magazines from Hong Kong and the Middle East, written for young people in general, sold on the news stands and the most popular magazines of their type, as their circulation proves.

■ **Self-supporting local churches**
Most local churches around the world are self-supporting – they pay for their own ministers and places of worship. But many still find this difficult and need subsidy from other churches, often through a central fund into which member churches pay. In India, my local church contributed the most to the central fund. In England it is subsidised from the fund.

■ **Financial stewardship** 'Northern' churches are overwhelmingly richer, because of the world economic situation. Many give generously and try to live responsibly. But many others around the world also give sacrificially and generously. There are also churches in poorer economies who spend lavishly on their own buildings or facilities. Stewardship is not a monopoly of any region.

■ **Cultural integrity** Many churches planted in the last 200 years suffer from 'cultural overhang'. They reflect the culture of those who started them. The problem here is obvious. It is often more subtle in older churches. They have also become a sub-culture, cut off from the social and intellectual mainstream of their culture, speaking only to fellow-Christians, often middle-class, out of touch with 'working class' or youth cultures.

■ **Minority situations** In some countries the church is a tiny minority. Its members may actually be 'second class' citizens, facing discrimination or pressure, unable to find social or economic status. Even if they are not, they may develop a 'minority complex', and become preoccupied with survival and community affairs. Despite this, many churches do have an impact on their society.
By contrast, western churches have a

long Christian heritage (even if today they are a minority, or seen as irrelevant). There are Christians in most walks of life, politics, professions, business, education, the arts (probably fewer in manual or industrial work).
It is possible to uphold Christian values, even if they have been eroded and need to be fought for. Pluralism is a key issue, but the Christian 'deposit' is still significant. The same is true of other countries or regions where Christians are a substantial part of the population.

■ **Leadership** Outstanding leaders are found all round the world. But where the proportion of Christians in society is small there is a smaller pool to draw from. Christian leaders in these situations face great pressures and are often lonely.

■ **Patterns of ministry** Freedom and tradition, innovation and bondage to hierarchies or 'one-man ministries' – these are found everywhere. No region has a monopoly!

■ **Theological reflection** It took the early church more than 300 years to hammer out its faith in relation to surrounding philosophies and cultures. Compared to that, churches in Asia and Africa are doing well, as they struggle with similar issues in their context. Western churches have been based on work done over centuries in their culture. They have also developed strong tools for biblical scholarship.
But all that is changing. The challenges of pluralism or poverty or environmental issues are universal. So liberation theologies from Latin America, or African cultural expressions of the gospel, or Asian wrestlings with other faiths, all contribute to the world church's theological task.

Becoming world Christians

So where does the balance lie? Which churches are strong and which are weak? Which churches need to help the others?
You can decide for yourself. There are strengths and weaknesses on all sides, some in surprising places. It sounds a cliche, but what we need is inter-dependence, and genuine partnership. We need to share resources, in all directions.
How do we do that? That's part of what this book is all about.
So should we go on talking about the 'Third World'? Why can't we just talk about the world – God's world? And seek to become world Christians.

CULTURE to CULTURE

THE WORLD CHRISTIAN

Unit 2

MISSIONARIES
A THREATENED SPECIES?

CONTENTS

PURPOSE

PART A The purpose of this unit is to help you to assess the western missionary movement of the past 300 years. You will look at four major criticisms of missionary activity. You will also consider whether missionaries are needed today and become aware of today's global missionary movement.

PART B You will discover more of the missionary history (past and present) of the church in one region of the world.

The opening quotations are from *The Bible and the Flag* by Brian Stanley (Apollos 1990) — pages 11, 70, 11 and 157 respectively. The book is a careful study of the relationship between Protestant missions and British imperialism in the 19th and 20th centuries. This book has been used as the main source for this unit.

MISSIONARIES UNDER ATTACK

The 'modern' missionary movement has taken place during the last 300 years. Here are four popular views about what the missionaries achieved.

> I go back to Africa to try to make an open path for commerce and Christianity.
>
> DAVID LIVINGSTONE, 4th DECEMBER 1857

> The missionaries came to Africa with "the Bible in one hand and the gun in the other."

> It has been alleged with truth that the trader and the settler followed the missionary, who was the agent of European imperialism.
>
> N. PITYANA, 1973

> Historians, anthropologists and theologians unite in their judgement that missionaries have been guilty of foisting their own cultural values on their converts.

Awkward questions

As we saw in unit 1, the Christian church exists today in every country around the world. It has spread because of the work of missionaries

FOUR CRITICISMS

There are several criticisms implied in the quotations above:

1 Missionaries were agents (whether conscious or not) of the forces of colonial and imperial expansion from the West.

2 Missionaries worked hand in hand with commercial interests, seeking to exploit the vast new markets opening up for them.

3 Missionaries did not just preach Christianity but also imposed their own culture, ignoring or destroying the cultural traditions they found.

A further criticism, which has not been mentioned yet, is even more fundamental:

4 Missionaries were arrogant because they believed that they were right and others were wrong. They claimed that Christianity was true and other religions and world views were false.

... and thirdly...

over the centuries. The fact is undeniable. But is it a good thing?

The British broadcaster Julian Pettifer is one of those who has questions. *Missionaries* was the title of his major BBC TV series and book (early 1990). They set out to explore 'what motivates these extraordinary men and women who go to the ends of the earth in search of converts…'

The implication of his study seemed to be that the motives of missionaries were very mixed. Colonialism, commerce, cultural change and Christianity were all part of the same package.

These criticisms are widespread, not only among those who are not Christian, but in many churches as well. Look at the box on the opposite page. You may have heard them all and thought about them yourself. You may also have other questions and criticisms to add to these. If so, note them here:

Answering the questions

Most of our perception of missionaries and missionary work is based on the last 300 years and especially the 19th century. The focus is on *western* missionaries, from European and North American countries.

This is, of course, a limited perspective. There have always been missionaries from other countries, as we shall see later in this unit. But we cannot avoid focussing for the moment on the western missionary movement, because of its influence on the way we look at mission.

How do we assess missionaries? Did they export their cultures? Were they just the agents of imperialism and commercial gain? Did they liberate people or exploit them? Has the missionary movement been a good thing or bad? Should we look back with regret at the 'Vasco da Gama era' of the church (and the West)?

More important – do we need missionaries today? If so, what should be their role?

People will assess these questions differently according to their background and presuppositions. However, our background and presuppositions are not enough to go on.

> What is of supreme importance is that these several assessments should be based on truth and not mythology, on evidence rather than propaganda.
>
> STANLEY, PAGE 13

Easier said than done! But we will try.

LOOKING AHEAD

In this unit we will look at two aspects of the missionary question:

■ **The past** First we will look back at the last 300 years or so of the modern missionary movement. We will try to assess the four criticisms listed above.

■ **The present** Then we will look at what is happening today. We will try to answer these questions: Do we need missionaries today? If so, what kind?

First came the Explorers...

then the Conquerors...

then the Missionaries...

and finally the Wheeler-Dealers.

GOSPEL AND EMPIRE

The year was 1497. The Portuguese explorer Vasco da Gama left Portugal and sailed around the Cape of Good Hope in search of a new route to the Indies – and the spices and other goods that Europe wanted so much.

It was the beginning of a new age for Europeans, the discovery of new worlds – the New World itself, but also Asia, Africa, Australia and the islands of the Pacific.

The empires

It was also the beginning of colonial and commercial expansion, sometimes deliberate, sometimes almost accidental.

The growth of the British Empire, for example, was a complex and haphazard phenomenon, with no apparent plan and many factors involved. These included curiosity, greed, rivalry with other European powers, strategic considerations, requests for help, concern for the welfare of people facing oppression and injustice and – at a fairly late stage – the conviction that European civilisation was something good to be shared with others.

The result: vast areas of the world were colonised by the various European powers. Not all. Japan, for example, welcomed the fascinating foreigners at first, but then became afraid of their aggressive tendencies and closed its doors until the end of the 19th century.

Enter the gospel

Almost simultaneously, the Christian gospel began to expand outwards from Europe, which had received it centuries earlier. First came the Roman Catholics, to South America and parts of Asia. Protestants were much slower, not really starting until the end of the 17th century. William Carey did not reach India until 1793,

just 200 years ago.

In some places, like South America, the connection was explicit. Christianity and conquest were part of the same package. Elsewhere it was not so clear and in some cases colonialism and Christianity seemed to be opposing forces. For example, early pioneers like William Carey and Adoniram Judson were not allowed to land in the territory of the East India Company. But by the end of the 19th century the dominance of Europe was the dominance of Christian Europe, of 'Christian civilisation'.

Into the 20th century

The 20th century changed all that. Two world wars – essentially European civil wars – brought the collapse of European power and any claim to moral superiority. The rise of Communism challenged Western powers with a force equally committed to control the world (or to liberate it?). And new currents of thought within Western culture had eroded Christian beliefs and presuppositions. Darwin, Freud and Marx, the giants of the 19th century, decisively shaped the way we look at the world today.

The colonial empires broke up. One by one the nations emerged, some with new names, and took their places at the United Nations. Between 1942 and 1984 almost 100 countries became independent.

Of course economic domination is another matter. Many people argue that it is more powerful and far-reaching than the old colonialism. Today's imperial powers are the commercial empires and unbridled spending power of the 'North', or of the oil-rich countries, or of the rich elites in poorer countries.

End of history lesson!

BETWEEN 1942 AND 1984 ALMOST

COUNTRIES BECAME INDEPENDENT

The end of the missionary era?

But what happened to the gospel and the churches which had been planted now in almost every country of the world?

Many assumed that independence from the colonial powers would mean the end of the missionary enterprise and the disappearance of the churches started by them.

This did not happen. In some cases the churches grew stronger than before. In others they seemed to be struggling with the legacies of the past. But they certainly did not disappear. Even in China, where it seemed that the tide of Communism and the Cultural Revolution of the late 1960s had swept away everything connected with the colonial past, the church has now emerged many times stronger than it was before.

Many of the new leaders of independent countries (especially in Africa) were the products of missionary education and training. Their sense of nationalism was largely the product of Western liberal democratic ideas, which were themselves at least in part based on Christian values.

So they were not entirely negative towards Christianity, just as they did not reject everything from the colonial past. In most cases, there was no immediate reaction against the missionary movement.

However, that began to change. *The Bible and the Flag* describes how all the questions we have raised came into sharp focus during the past 40 years or so, precisely as a result of the massive changes taking place in countries that had previously been colonies.

These included political changes, sometimes towards authoritarian rule, ideological and economic issues, theological trends and changes within the churches.

ESSENTIAL MISSIONARY EQUIPMENT?

FIVE FACTORS FOR CHANGE

Here are five factors which brought about a changed view of missions in the post-colonial ferment. (These are taken from *The Bible and the Flag*.)

1. Conflict between church and state in Africa

Some early leaders, like Dr Kwame Nkrumah of Ghana, began as great champions of freedom but later became authoritarian, and in some cases, dictators. This sometimes led to clashes with Christians who resisted such trends. As a result, these early leaders tended to be critical of the church and its missionary background.

2. Marxist influence

The growth of Marxist influence, especially in Africa, gave an alternative view of the world to the Christian view. This was highly critical of colonialism, and usually linked it with the role of religion, 'the opiate of the people'. It seemed highly plausible to see Christian mission as the hand-maid of imperialism.

3. Dependency and neo-colonialism

People soon realised that freedom from colonialism did not automatically lead to economic development. In fact things often seemed to be worse. Was this just the slow road to 'modernisation'? Or was it because the capitalist powers still had control? Were they deliberately keeping the rest of the world in dependency – turning it into what would soon be called the Third World? Was this a new, more subtle form of colonialism?

Such views became widespread. And it was natural to see foreign missionaries from the same perspective, still controlling the purse strings even if they were not actually in charge.

4. The rise of indigenous theologies

Asian theology, African theology, Black theology, Liberation theology – these were all efforts to look at the Gospel in a fresh way, freeing it from the 'cultural imperialism' of Western theology. Could the Gospel be expressed in an African way, for example? If so, what aspects of African tradition and culture could be included? What Western elements would need to be discarded?

These were the questions. The answers were very varied and the debate still goes on! But it naturally led to serious questioning about the role of western missionaries and the apparent foreignness of Christianity.

5. The ecumenical movement

The ecumenical movement brought churches together from across the world. 'Older' and 'younger' churches now met as equals. It was exciting. But it also meant that a lot of time and effort was put into working out the relationship, sometimes with a lot of tension. There was an attempt to move from 'missions' to 'mission'.

Alongside this, the agenda of the World Council of Churches from the sixties onwards was largely taken from what was happening in the world around: human rights, the search for equality and dignity, freedom from exploitation, the ending of colonial rule, the clash of political ideologies, the passionate search for justice and freedom from hunger.

MISSIONARIES GO HOME!

Look at the *Five Factors for Change* box on page 21, which describes five factors that led to a changed view of missions at the end of the colonial era. What was the effect of all these trends?

Imagine that you had been a Christian living through the fifties or sixties in a newly independent country. How do you think you would have felt about foreign missionaries? What changes would you like to have seen in their relationship with your church?

> **"When African historians come to write their own account of the adventure of Africa with imperialism, they will write of the missionaries as the greatest friends the African had."**
> A statement made by a Nigerian politician in 1947.

What do you think would have been the main problems or issues? How would you have solved them?

Reactions were in fact very mixed. Some were predictably very negative about the whole missionary enterprise. Others were surprisingly positive.

In the 1970s, some people called for a moratorium on foreign missionary activity…

KENYA 1971

All foreign missionaries should be withdrawn for at least five years, says the Revd John Gatu, an evangelical Presbyterian minister.

This will free the African churches from the bondage of Western dependency and enable them to discover their selfhood.

BANGKOK 1973

The conference on 'Salvation Today' endorsed the call for a moratorium on missionary funds and personnel. 'The missionary era has ended and the era of world mission has just begun' said Emilio Castro, new director of the Commission on World Mission and Evangelism.

Many delegates feel this is the only way to end old forms of mission and so be free to engage in the really urgent tasks – to feed the hungry, release the prisoners, bring justice to the world; in other words 'Salvation Today', not tomorrow.

What do you think about the call for a moratorium? How would you have responded...

■ if you had been an African Christian in the 1970s?

■ if you had been an expatriate missionary in Africa in the 1970s?

The moratorium call brought much heart-searching on all sides. Was it a serious call to stop all funds and personnel – or was it just an expression of frustration at continuing dependency? Was it realistic in the light of current needs?

Should missionaries go home, or should they rather move on to new, unevangelised areas?

Many missionaries were involved in institutional work in hospitals, schools, training and development programmes. Moving on might not be very practical. At the very least it would mean accelerating the transfer of control to local Christians.

In India the debate did not generate as much interest, partly because the Indian government had controlled the entry of foreign missionaries from the early fifties. The Anglican church had had its first Indian bishop in 1907 (V.S. Azariah) and the churches as a whole had gone much further in developing relationships of equality and partnership.

The Lausanne Congress, 1974

Latin Americans raised the issue from a different angle. At the Lausanne Congress on World Evangelisation in 1974, they spoke out against the cultural dominance of foreign missionaries and churches. They felt that this could lead to a distortion of the Gospel.

The 'Lausanne Covenant' responded to that concern and also referred briefly to the moratorium debate: 'A reduction of foreign missionaries and money in an evangelised country may sometimes be necessary to facilitate the national church's growth in self-reliance and to release resources for unevangelised areas.'

Notice here the positive emphasis on 'moving on' rather than 'going home'.

The World Council of Churches urged its members to be free from 'selfishness in sharing with one another our resources...'

The issue today

By the 1980s the moratorium issue had almost faded away. The main concern had been achieved – to assert the independence and self-reliance of younger churches and their responsibility for mission in their own country.

The larger debate – what mission is really all about – continues to this day!

WERE THEY WRONG?

What do we make of the western missionary movement of the past 300 years? Let's look again at the four criticisms:

1. Keeping the flag flying?

'Missionaries were agents (conscious or not) of the forces of colonial and imperial expansion from the West'. True or False?

Brian Stanley's book is really a study of this statement. You need to read the whole book (and probably several more) to discuss it properly! He concludes, as we might expect, that there is no simple answer.

As we have already seen, the growth of the British Empire was haphazard. Missionaries also had different attitudes to the empire:

■ Some saw it as providing a way for the gospel (as the Roman Empire did in the 1st century).
■ Some also believed that it had a civilising mission to other peoples. They saw this as part of God's providence.
■ Others disagreed and opposed the whole idea of empire.
■ Many found themselves in conflict from time to time with the colonial powers on specific issues. See the box for examples.

It is impossible to do justice to all the different points of view here. But Brian Stanley's comment seems fair:
The missionaries 'only rarely questioned or opposed the fact of British imperial rule; but they consistently challenged and criticised the morality with which it operated, with particular regard to its treatment of subject peoples. The missionary calling was to keep the flag in check, not to haul it down.' (p.179).

On the other hand 'what has made the greatest negative impression on the collective memory of Christians in the former colonies are... the countless instances where individual missionaries have displayed arrogance, insensitivity and lack of trust...'

MISSIONARIES IN CONFLICT

■ John Smith, a Congregational missionary in the West Indies, was condemned to death in 1823 for opposing slavery in the plantations.

■ William Carey's colleagues, along with Indian leaders, campaigned against *sati* in India and persuaded the British governor of Bengal to abolish it in 1829.

■ In Kenya missionaries campaigned against unjust land and labour laws in the 1920s, spoke out against 'white supremacy', and affirmed human equality.

But this is 'only to acknowledge that missionaries... have been fallible men and women of their own time, sharing in the prejudices of the social groups from which they came.' (p.182).

Something for all of us to think about there?

Think about your own church or group. Do you think you share the 'prejudices of the social groups' which you come from? In what ways?

Do you think you would need to change or adapt in any way in another culture?

2. Prophecy and profits?

'Missionaries worked hand in hand with commercial interests, seeking to exploit the vast new markets opening up for them.' True or false?

'I go back to Africa to try to make an open path for commerce and Christianity.'

David Livingstone's famous statement is often quoted to show the explicit connection between Christianity and commercial exploitation. However, this interpretation takes his words completely out of context.

Livingstone and many others believed that the greatest evil threatening Africa was the slave trade. They saw legitimate commerce as the best way to cut it off at its source. The Sierra Leone Company was founded in 1790 with this as its first aim. It was one of many such ventures, not only in Africa.

Missionaries believed that legitimate trade was good in itself. For some it was part of the process of bringing change and 'civilisation'. But they could also be critical of trade based only on the desire for profit – the slave trade of course, the opium trade in China, uncontrolled free-trade in India, or the sale of firearms and liquor, which did so much damage in many places.

Livingstone was aware of the limitations of commerce, as the quote on the right shows.

Do you think that trade and Christianity are compatible?

"Commerce has the effect of speedily letting the tribes see their mutual dependence... It is so far good. But Christianity alone reaches the very centre of the wants of Africa and of the world...You will see I appreciate the effects of commerce much, but those of Christianity much more."
David Livingstone

Today many churches and missions are heavily involved in what is called 'development' – through social involvement, aid, agriculture, education and many other ways.

Was the emphasis on commerce in the 18th and 19th centuries similar to the emphasis on development today? What are the strengths and limitations of such an approach?

Some missionaries (but not all) come from cultures with better technology and higher economic status than the people they go to. What do you think are the
■ advantages
■ disadvantages
of being in such a position?

What about the opposite situation, where the missionary is not so advanced technologically or economically?

3. Cultural imperialism?

'Missionaries did not just preach Christianity but also imposed their own culture, ignoring or destroying the cultural traditions they found.' True or false?

It is easy to laugh at pictures of missionaries dressing their converts in baggy shorts or black suits and teaching them Victorian table manners.

There is no doubt that the majority considered that part of the benefit of Christianity was that it would change and improve people's way of life in every aspect. Many explicitly directed (sometimes even imposed) the changes they thought were right.

So drums were forbidden, or clothes and diet changed (Christians became known in India as 'beef-eaters'). Church buildings and ways of worship would often reflect the pattern 'at home', with pipe organs (or harmoniums), pews and translated hymns.

The amazing growth of African independent churches in recent years is one indication of people's reaction against this and their desire to express their own culture.

But it is dangerous to oversimplify the issue of culture. Look at the material in the margin.

What do you think missionaries should have done? Choose the best option(s) below:

■ Preach the gospel and leave people to discover the cultural implications for themselves.
■ Help new Christians to work out a Christian way of life within their own culture.
■ Tell converts how the gospel should be applied to their situation.
■ Separate their preaching entirely from people's culture and way of life.
■ Any other suggestions?

The issue is still very relevant! We can easily assume that American culture, or Korean, Tamil, Nigerian, Brazilian, or .... is the most Christian...

How do we decide? We will return to this question in Unit 5.

4. Is it true?

'Missionaries were arrogant because they believed they were right and others were wrong. They claimed that Christianity was true and other religions and world views were false.' True or false?

Missionaries have made all kinds of mistakes. They are fallible human beings, after all.

But one thing is clear. For all their mistakes, their over-riding motivation was not the growth of empire, or the advancement of civilisation. It was the conviction that they had a message which was universal and compelling. God had revealed Himself uniquely in Jesus Christ. And so all must submit to his Lordship and respond to his love.

Were they arrogant?

The idea that one view is right and others wrong is very hard for modern people to accept. So anybody claiming to have a 'true' message is automatically suspect. They will appear to be arrogant.

Is Christianity 'true'? In what sense? Is it the only 'truth'? These questions are too big for us to discuss here. We will come back to them (along with all the others) in Unit 5.

So our judgment about missionary 'arrogance' will have to wait. It is connected with our view of truth.

GOSPEL & CULTURE

Here are three points to consider when thinking through how the gospel and human culture affect each other.

1. There were some missionaries who realised the problem of unnecessary and superficial change:
'We think that the great object (of preaching the gospel) is not the changing of the names, the dress, the food, and the innocent usages of mankind, but to produce a moral and divine change in the hearts and conduct of men' (William Carey and his colleagues in India, 1806). Some showed great sensitivity in allowing the gospel to spread within existing cultural patterns – for example among the Mizos of north-east India.

2. It is impossible to separate the gospel from its effects on the whole of life. If it is not applied to all areas, it implies that Christ is not Lord of all our lives. The 'moral and divine change' which Carey and his colleagues longed for will bring other changes in other aspects as well. In this sense missionaries were right to expect the gospel to bring change.
The question is: What kind of change and what will be the model? Should it be the missionary's own culture?

3. Missionaries were not the only agents of change. The world was dominated by the impact of European exploration, acquisition and technology. Change was inevitable as a result. The choice forced upon many peoples was not whether to change, but in which direction.

MISSIONARIES TODAY?

The figures used on the following pages are taken from Larry Pate's book *From Every People: Missionaries from the Two Thirds World*, MARC Publications, 1989. Some other sources give lower figures. Even so, the growth is undeniable and remarkable.

One reason for the different figures is the question: how do you define 'missionary'? 80% of those included work *within* their own country, but with people of different languages and cultures. They are clearly cross-cultural workers.

But what about those who work in another region, or even country, but with people of their own culture? What about those who work with south Indians in north India, or with Japanese in Bolivia? Should they be included?

The reason why so many work in their own country is primarily because of the need and opportunity there, but also because of the practical difficulty for many countries of sending currency abroad.

THE TOP 2 MISSIONARY AGENCIES OF THE NON-WESTERN WORLD TODAY ARE...

THE BURMA BAPTIST CONVENTION. NUMBER OF MISSIONARIES:

1440

AND THE DIOCESAN MISSIONARY ASSOCIATION OF KENYA. NUMBER OF MISSIONARIES:

1283

Do we need missionaries today? Here are two answers that are often given to this question:

> No! It's better to close off that era. Enough damage has been done. Look at the criticisms we've just been discussing. Let's leave people alone in their ways. There's so much <u>we</u> have to learn from <u>them</u>!

A COMMON ANSWER, INCLUDING FROM SOME CHRISTIANS

> No — on balance we probably don't need them. The church exists around the world. It's better to leave it to them to evangelise their own people. They can avoid the sort of mistakes we have discussed. They don't have to cross cultural barriers. It's probably more economical.

ANOTHER ANSWER, PROBABLY MORE COMMON AMONG CHRISTIANS

What do you think? Do you agree with either of the views above? Or do you have another?

Look at the first speech bubble above. It's difficult to give a complete response just now to this viewpoint. We would need to look more at what the Bible says about mission. We will do that in Units 3 and 4.

It also raises large questions about the truth of what we believe and our attitude to other faiths. We will look at these questions again in Unit 5.

So for the moment we will have to leave that answer in suspense.

The viewpoint expressed in the second speech bubble contains some

truth. It is vital that the church in each place should take the responsibility for evangelism of the people in its own area and culture.

But there are two very important facts which this answer does not take into account:

1. A church for every people

Let us assume that the Christian faith is true and universal. Then we need to remember what we said in Unit 1 about individuals and 'people groups'. Look back at page 11 and remind yourself…

> ■ what is a 'people group'?
> ■ how would the gospel spread within such a group?

Once there is a church within a people group, the gospel can spread without crossing further cultural barriers.

But the fact is, as we saw, that there are millions of individuals and thousands of people groups who have either not heard about Christ at all, or who do not have a viable church among their own people. In other words, they have no one from whom they can receive the gospel *in their own culture*.

In Unit 1 we looked at very broad statistics, of countries and continents. They give some idea of the overall situation. But they can be misleading. You probably felt frustrated with some of the figures in Unit 1. They didn't seem to match your local situation.

These kind of figures need to be broken up into the many different cultures and sub-cultures, languages and social groupings which they represent.

There may be churches in every country. Some may be growing fast. But there are still unreached social,cultural and linguistic sub-groups of people for whom there is no indigenous community of believing Christians, able to evangelise their own people.

Somebody will have to cross cultural barriers in order to bring them the Gospel in their own culture and language. It may be those nearest to them culturally. Or it may be somebody from a completely different culture. One factor in our world is the political barriers which sometimes deny entry to people of one citizenship, while welcoming another passport.

2. God's multi-coloured pattern

Something new is happening today. We have been looking so far at the modern missionary movement from Europe and then North America. For better or for worse, that is where most of the missionaries of the past 300 years have come from. And we have seen how the expansion of Christianity has been linked with (but not identical to) the expansion of western power.

However, that is rapidly changing.

It has always been true that missionaries have not been exclusively European or American. The first Christian missionaries were Asian and African – it was only later that Europeans joined in! A lot of early Christian outreach was towards the East. It was a long time before Europe became Christian.

In the last 200 years also there have been outstanding examples of non-Western missionaries, as we shall see.

But the last 20 years have seen a phenomenal growth of missionaries and mission agencies from the non-western countries of Asia, Africa, Latin America and Oceania, up to an estimated 35,000 Protestant missionaries today, working in 118 countries of the world.

That compares with about 85,000 from western countries (of whom about 30,000 are short-term workers). The numbers have grown very fast as the chart on page 30 shows.

PEOPLE GROUPS AND YOU

Can you think of any such people groups known to you…

■ in your country or area? (What about youth sub-cultures? Or people of different cultures or races? Or even different social classes?)

■ in other countries or areas that are accessible to you?

Is anybody working among them?

What would you call them? (The name 'missionary' raises questions for many. We will discuss some of these questions in Unit 7.)

WORLD MISSION

THE TOP TEN

The Top Ten sending countries of the non-western world in 1988 were as follows. The number indicates active missionaries.

India: 8905
Nigeria: 2959
Zaire: 2731
Burma: 2560
Kenya: 2242
Brazil: 2040
Philippines: 1814
Ghana: 1545
Zimbabwe: 1540
Korea: 1184

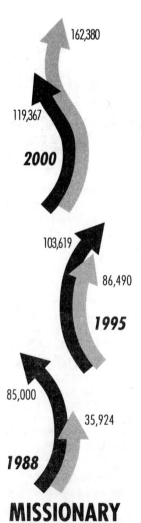

162,380

119,367

2000

103,619

86,490

1995

85,000

35,924

1988

MISSIONARY GROWTH

Black arrows represent the western world. Grey arrows the non-western world.

The modern story began in the 19th century. Here are just a few examples…

■ **Burma and Thailand** Back in 1833, the Karens of Burma, who had only recently been evangelised, began outreach to the Kachin, a very different people, as well as to other Karens in Thailand. The Burma Baptist Convention is still the largest single missionary agency in Asia.

■ **Tongans** planted the church in Fiji in 1835. Their King sent a message to the paramount chief of Fiji, preparing the way for a group of Tongan missionaries! British missionaries joined the partnership later in the same year. Well over 1,000 missionaries have been sent between the many islands of the Pacific since then, many travelling from island to island in their deep-sea canoes.

■ **Jamaicans** began missionary work in Cameroon in 1893. They started Bible translation, printing and education. Today Caribbean Christians from Britain continue to work in Ghana, Nigeria, Liberia and other West African countries.

■ **Latin American** countries have been sending missionaries within their continent, as well as to Spain, Portugal and the USA. COMIBAM, a congress on mission in São Paulo in 1987, gave a new push to send missionaries outside the continent. There is a special interest in working in the Muslim countries of North Africa and the Middle East.

A Brazilian girl heard about Asians from Hindu and Muslim backgrounds. She came to London to learn English and is now working with south Asians in Manchester.

■ **India** India's missionary movement goes back to 1884, when the Methodist Church sent a missionary to Singapore. The Indian Missionary society was founded in 1903, followed soon after by the National Missionary Society. Both are still active. But the explosion of missionary growth began in the fifties and sixties. Individuals, churches and small groups began to go, or dream about going, to unreached areas of north India. 'Go or Send' was the motto of one of the groups. Today their efforts have grown into thousands of cross-cultural workers all over India, and abroad as well. A marine biologist from Madras left his research to work with students in Thailand. Teachers have gone to Fiji and other Pacific Islands, medical workers to Afghanistan, evangelists and pastors to Britain.

■ **Japan** In the 1960s three young Japanese went to India for theological study. Their purpose: to learn another language and culture and prepare for overseas missionary work. They went back to Japan, married three sisters and scattered again to work in India and the

Caribbean. Other Japanese work today in Kenya, Indonesia, Nepal, Thailand, Britain, and at least 20 other countries.

■ **Korea** A Korean girl works in London with Bengali Muslims and Burmese Buddhists. A theological student is now pastor to Korean businessmen in Bombay. A dentist has a clinic and plans for a dental college in Northern China. Koreans in the Middle East make an impression with their early morning prayer meetings.

■ **Africans** cross national and cultural boundaries within their continent. Kenyan students in India have a powerful witness. Nigerians and Ghanaians in Britain evangelise the local people. The East African Revival has ministered to people all round the world.

Reflection

What do you think about the missionary movement of today? Did anything surprise you?

What answer do you want to give now to the question: Do we need missionaries today? Look back to page 28. Do you want to modify your answer there in any way?

> *"For the first time in history, the good news is truly becoming a gospel from every people!"*
> *Larry Pate*

WORKING ON YOUR OWN?

If you are working on your own, write down your answers to B and C of the Group Activity material (see page 34).

WHAT NOW?

How do we respond to this new missionary movement? Here are three suggestions:

1. Thank God for what he is doing.

It is truly exciting to see the multi-coloured pattern which God is creating, of missionaries from every country and culture to every country and culture.

2. Learn the lessons of the past.

We have seen the mistakes that missionaries from the West have made over the past 300 years. For all their achievements, they did find it difficult sometimes to disentangle the gospel from their culture, from commercial interests, or from colonial expansion.

But it's always easier to see the mistakes that others have made in the past than the ones that we are making now. We need to look carefully at ourselves to make sure that we have really learned from the past and are not just repeating it.

3. Join in!

Recognise and be part of this global and international missionary movement.

It is God's way of showing Christ as the universal Lord. We live in a world which is a market place of ideas and values. Buddhism, Hinduism, Islam, Marxism, materialism – and many others – compete for our hearts and minds. The multinationals have spread the gospel of Coca Cola to the corners of the planet. Petrodollars have helped to export and establish Islam from West to East. The New Age movement is diffusing the spiritual and social values of Hinduism and Eastern philosophy around the world.

Each of these wants to be seen as the universal faith. We have discovered the truth in Christ, or rather we have been discovered by him. We know that he is the Way for all. But for many, Christ is a western figure for western people (even though rejected by many of them) just as Buddha, Krishna and others are for their own people. They will acknowledge him as universal Lord only when they see him incarnated and brought to them by men and women from all races and cultures.

Christians from growing and vibrant churches anywhere in the world can and must have a mission to the secularised and empty people of the West or the East. They can help them to adjust to a pluralist, multi-faith, multi-racial society. They can help to counteract the influence of the gurus, the cults and pseudo-religions. They can teach affluent Christians about living in a world of poverty and inequality.

GROUP ACTIVITY

A. Were they wrong?

1. Ask the group to share their responses to the four criticisms (pages 24–27).

2. What can we learn from the mistakes – and achievements – of the past?

This discussion could go on a long time, so you will need to limit it in order to give time for B and C below.

B. Do we need missionaries today?

To answer this question, divide the group into pairs. Ask half the pairs to discuss question 1 below. The other half should discuss question 2.

1. Do you think you need to *receive* missionaries from another country or culture in your country and your church? Why or why not?

If so, what kind of missionaries would you like to see? List some of the *roles* they could fulfil and the personal *qualities and skills* they would need, on the chart. (Underline *receive*; cross out *send*.)

2. Do you think that the church or churches in your country should *send* missionaries to other countries or to people of another culture in your country? Why or why not?

If so, what kind of missionaries would you like to send? List some of the *roles* they could fulfil and the personal *qualities and skills* they would need, on the chart. (Underline *send*, cross out *receive*.)

3. After 10 minutes, compare the answers from the two sets of pairs. Are they similar? If there are differences, what do you think are the reasons?

C. God's multi-coloured pattern

Do you know any missionaries either from western or from non-western countries or cultures? Or from both backgrounds?

What do you think are the
■ advantages and opportunities
■ disadvantages and limitations
of missionaries from either background?

What can they learn from each other?

D. Conclusion

In the light of your discussion, what practical suggestions would you make to...
■ your own congregation or group?
■ your church leaders?
■ individual missionaries whom you know?
■ missionary societies with whom you are in touch?

Close your session with a time of prayer:
■ thank God for what he is doing in the world.
■ pray for missionaries you know.
■ pray for changes needed to make the missionary movement truly worldwide.

The missionaries we would like to

RECEIVE / SEND

Qualities and skills they need:

Roles they could fulfil:

GOING FURTHER

Where did the church come from?

In Unit 1 we found out about the church in another region of the world – its similarities and differences from the local churches we know. Now look at its missionary situation:

How did the gospel come to that region? What is the situation today? Are the churches there *receiving* missionaries? Are they *sending* missionaries?

Begin by reading the history of mission in that region. The best short account is found in *Ripening Harvest, Gathering Storm*, pp.41–93. Look for the pages which deal with the region you are studying, in earlier as well as later periods. If you can read the whole section it will give you a fascinating survey of the church's mission from the beginning until now.

The Seoul Declarations

Asia has seen at least two major congresses on mission, both in Seoul. Look at the extracts on page 34 from their two Declarations. What do you learn from them about mission in the Asian church?

■ What is the attitude to missionaries from the past? What are the positive and negative comments?
■ Do you notice any differences between the two Declarations? Can you think of reasons? Compare the respective dates.
■ What is the attitude of the participants to mission today? Whose responsibility is it?
■ What differences would you expect to see in the Asian church and around the world over the next 10 years, as a result?

Write a brief 'press release', reporting on the 1990 congress for your church or group. The report could be for your magazine or noticeboard, or given verbally.

For Registered Students

A. Write a brief report on the history and present status of mission in the region you are studying. This should include…

■ major events or periods in the spread of Christianity in the region.
■ the present situation: missionaries received, missionaries sent.

Present your material as in Unit 1.

B. Write the analysis of the Seoul Declarations described above and turn it into a 'press release', as suggested.

C. Send your work to your tutor with a report on how you presented the material. Describe the place, date, type of group and the response you received.

Send your work within two weeks of doing this Unit. That should give you enough time to get some response.

OTHER USEFUL SOURCES

Operation World
A History of Christian Missions, Stephen Neill, Pelican 1964 – the definitive 'short history'.
The Quiet Revolution, pp.303-311.

THE SEOUL DECLARATIONS

AUGUST 1975

Facts:

- All Asia Mission Consultation
- 300 participants and observers from 16 countries
- Organised by Asia Missions Association

We have paved a new, broad road linking the East and West, the North and South in Christian mission, unlike the old, restricted, one-way road of mission from the West (Isaiah 62:10)...

We gratefully salute the numerous heroic pioneers of Christian mission who dedicated their lives not only for the sake of saving souls in many nations, but also for the sake of assisting the peoples of those nations in solving basic human problems...

Nevertheless we are compelled to point out honestly that the territorial expansion, commercialism, imperialism and colonialism of Western nations often have been stumbling blocks in presenting the core of the Gospel to the oppressed peoples of the Third World...

At the same time, we humbly recognise and repent of our own failures and mistakes. We Christians in the Third World often have been over-dependent upon the Western churches. We have been too slow to realise our responsibility to share the missionary vision. We have been even blaming the Western church for our own deficiencies and failures...

Has the Western Christian missionary enterprise accomplished its goal and come to an end, as the advocates of moratorium insist? We warn against such a hasty conclusion...

There are significant potential mission forces emerging from various countries of Asia, Africa and Latin America. We realise the urgency to mobilise and train these forces...

To carry out the heavy task of recruiting and training new mission forces requires long–term efforts, a close cooperation between East and West, and a tremendous expenditure of funds...

AUGUST 1990

Facts:

- Asia Missions Congress
- 1302 participants and observers from 50 countries
- Organised by Evangelical Fellowship of Asia

We look back in gratitude to the sacrificial and fruitful labours of missionaries, mostly from the West, who faithfully sowed the seed of the gospel through which the Church has been planted in our lands over the past 200 years.

While we have been disappointed by some of the cultural insensitivities of those who have brought the gospel to our lands, we confess we have been guilty of similar cultural domination in some of our own missionary endeavours.

We look to the present in praise to God for the growth and maturity of the Church in Asia. As evidence of this we rejoice in the rapid growth and development of the Asian missionary movement. We therefore renew our commitment to complete the task of world missions in reliance upon the Holy Spirit...

We commit ourselves: To make the Great Commission the primary focus of our personal ministry, and that of the churches and organisations we represent...

To do all possible to ensure that the cause of world evangelisation becomes an integral part of the life of every local church, association of churches and denomination...

To mobilise the entire membership of local congregations to pray, give and send or go regardless of their economic or political status...

To a partnership in world evangelisation within the body of Christ, to counteract the divisions that have often hindered us...

We expect a great harvest in this decade and, ultimately, the realisation of the Biblical vision of Revelation 7:9-10. '...a great multitude which no man could number, from every nation, from all tribes and peoples and tongues, standing before the throne and before the Lamb, clothed in white robes.'

THE WORLD CHRISTIAN

Unit 3

SELECTED TO SERVE

CONTENTS

PURPOSE

PART A The purpose of this unit is to help you to see the Bible's story as the story of mission. You will identify four major events in the biblical story and explain what the first three tell us about mission.

PART B You will explore some of these themes further.

THE BIBLE AND MISSION

Important questions

Something exciting is happening in our world today.

The church exists around the whole world – 'the great new fact of our era', as Archbishop William Temple described it.

A global missionary movement is under way, with people from every country crossing cultural barriers to share the good news.

But there are also questions and problems:

> ■ what about the effect of the gospel on other people's cultures?
> ■ what truth is there in other faiths? Do we affirm them or deny them?
> ■ is our mission primarily 'spiritual' or should we be equally concerned for social and material needs?
> ■ what is our ultimate goal: to change individuals or to transform the structures of society?

And so on...

The 'why' of mission

How do we know that we should even be involved? Are we just continuing old patterns? What is the real basis for our mission?

To that last question, you are probably ready to answer 'the Bible', and you are right. The Bible does provide the basis for mission and the starting point for trying to answer the questions we have raised.

But which parts? What would you quote if you were asked what basis the Bible gives for mission?

You have probably quoted the 'Great Commission' from Matthew 28:19: 'Go therefore and make disciples of all nations, baptising them and teaching them...'

Or the shorter version in Mark 16:15: 'Go into all the world and preach the gospel to the whole creation'.

Or you might have thought of John 3:16: 'God so loved the world...'

But the biblical basis for mission is not just a few texts, important and striking as they are. Mission is part of the Bible from Genesis to Revelation. In fact we could say that the Bible itself is based on the fact of God's mission.

The story of the Bible *is* the story of mission. Mission and the Bible are inextricably linked. So if we want to be involved in God's purpose for mission we need to be involved with the Bible.

The biblical story

How would you sum up the biblical story? Could you describe it in a few major events: four or five, or at the most six or seven?

Dr Chris Wright sums up the biblical story in four events. (See his book, *The Use of the Bible in Social Ethics*, Grove Booklets on Ethics No. 51). These four events are:

Now look at the material in the margin. It looks very simple! In fact, 'Redemption in History' includes several more key events, as we shall see below. But these four major events summarise the Bible's story, and the story of mission. Try to remember them. Repeat them to yourself, or write them down on a piece of paper.

Why is this important? Because the Bible is a story with a beginning and an end. It begins with creation and ends with new creation. In between comes the tragedy of the fall and then the long story of God's redemption in history.

We can't really understand 'what the Bible says' about any topic unless we look at the whole story and see what each part tells us. What do these four events tell us about the Bible's story, and about mission?

A. Creation and mission

'In the beginning, God created the heavens and the earth' (Genesis 1:1). The Bible begins with the breathtaking picture of one world, created by God, good and perfect.

What does this tell us about…

- God

- ourselves

- the world we live in

- God's purposes?

Creation

↓

Fall

↓

Redemption in History

↓

New Creation

List as many things as you can think of under these headings. Then compare your list with the one on page 39.

That's quite a lot to think about! You could spend the rest of this unit – or the whole book – digesting all the implications. You could think about how different all this is from the views of most people around us. For example:

- a materialist universe that evolved by chance
- an impersonal principle behind all reality – a kind of world-soul
- a God who is so different, so all-powerful that he cannot be personally concerned about individuals.

But you may be asking – what does this tell us about mission?

Creation tells us God's original purposes for his world. It shows us how rich and wide they are. Whenever we think about mission we must start from this broad perspective of creation. Otherwise our perspective is narrower than God's.

Creation is only part of the Bible's story, of course. But look at the questions on the next page. See what answers you can find from this part of the story.

FURTHER THINKING

For guidelines on how to use the Bible to understand mission, see Part B, page 50.

HEALING GOD'S CREATION

It's good – but is it mission?

What activities can we include in mission?

Nineteenth-century Christians in Britain campaigned successfully against the slave trade, particularly in Africa. (Some people justified it on the grounds that Africans were inferior human beings.) Missionaries in Africa continued to oppose the slave trade – now carried on by other groups. Some saw trade as the only alternative, to develop the resources of the continent and provide legitimate sources of income.

Missionaries in India found themselves confronting social evils – for example the practice of widow-burning (*sati*), or the exploitation of peasants by European indigo planters or local landlords.

Were these different groups right? Were their activities part of mission? What does creation have to say about these issues? Does it provide any basis to support or criticise their actions?

Can you think of situations today in which Christians are involved in 'temporal' or 'social' issues? Is this part of mission?

'God made the world with a purpose' – how do you think that purpose should be carried out in the world today? Is that part of mission?

WHAT DOES CREATION TELL US?

■ **God** Creation tells us first about the Creator. There is one God — he is sovereign, all-powerful, infinite. The created world, with its order and design, speaks of this infinite power and wisdom. Proverbs 3:19: 'The Lord by wisdom founded the earth...'

The Bible also tells us that he is personal. Genesis 1 and 2 speak of God's purposeful, reflective, intelligent action. He created by his word. And he relates personally to his creation, especially human beings.

■ **The world** The world is good. It has value, beauty and order. It is real, made by God for a purpose. The evil in the world was not originally there. It is because of human sin, not because of any evil in matter itself. The whole creation is dependent on God. Human beings have a responsibility to preserve and care for it.

■ **Humanity** Human beings are part of the creation, just like other animals. But they are the crown of creation. They are different because God has made them in his image — this is what makes us unique!

God's image includes man and woman. Human beings are social beings, made for relationships with each other.

Sex, marriage, the family, are all good gifts of God.

We are dependent on God. We find our true meaning only as created beings. We are morally responsible and accountable to God. God made us good. All humanity is one. All are equal. All have dignity. God made human beings to work, to rest, to be productive and creative, like him.

He has made us stewards to have dominion as his agents. ('Dominion' does not mean 'domination'). We are responsible for all the resources of the world — animal, vegetable and mineral — for their discovery, development and fair distribution.

■ **God's purpose** God made the world with a purpose — to be inhabited and cared for by humanity (Isaiah 45:12,18ff).

Creation is the beginning of history. It is not a mythical event, outside of space and time. The world has a beginning, so it will have an end. History moves in a direction, towards the final consummation of God's purposes.

B. The fall and mission

Creation gives us the starting point for mission: God's universal purpose for his world. All of life is part of his purpose. But you may not have been able to give simple answers to the questions above, because creation cannot be separated from its tragic sequel – the fall.

Think of all the positive affirmations we have just made about God's creation and its meaning for the earth and mankind. The fall turns all these into negatives. Write down some of the negative results of the fall:

Compare your list with the one on page 41.

Sin was a deliberate act of rebellion against a personal God, disobedience against his explicit command, an attempt to assert human independence and self-sufficiency in place of humble dependence. Sin is not just selfishness or ignorance of one's true nature.

This second stage of the biblical story demands realism from us as we look at our world. We hardly need reminders of the fact of sin in every dimension of our existence. It is naive to neglect them. But it is equally important to realise that this is the second stage. It is not God's original plan.

Hmm. Not as nice as Genesis Chapter 1.

GENESIS 3

GENESIS

THE FALL AND REDEMPTION

What's the point?

The hero of Albert Camus' famous novel *La Peste* (*The Plague*) is a young doctor fighting against an outbreak of plague in the Algerian city of Oran. The plague is bad enough. But as he struggles, he wonders what he is doing. The people believe that the plague is a judgement from God. If it comes from God, then what is the use of fighting it? One would be fighting against God…

The doctor reaches the conclusion that this view is absurd. He must struggle, but in order to express his true humanity, he has to go against the will of an inscrutable God…

What do you think? Do you agree with the young doctor? What does the biblical story of the fall tell us about his attempt to solve the problem of evil? What is missing from it?

The focus of mission

What about all the other hospitals (especially Christian ones) that fight disease all the time? Healing bodies or minds may be part of God's will, which they are doing. But is that all there is to mission? What else is needed?

That's it! We'll call it 'The Armchair Mission'.

What about healthy, affluent, well adjusted professional people, living decent lives with their families in comfortable suburbs all round the world? What is the nature of mission to them?

What does the fall add to our understanding of mission from creation?

Sin requires a remedy from outside mankind. Men and women cannot solve the problem of sin from within themselves. Only God can undo the effects of his judgement.

So mission must focus on the root of humanity's problem. Unless it does this it is missing the point.

How do we do this while still keeping the breadth of God's purpose for creation? That is a tension that always faces us in mission. Keep it in mind as we turn now to the third stage in the Bible's story.

C. Redemption in history and mission

Sin spoiled God's creation. But it did not stop God's purpose. The rest of the Bible is the story of God's redemption in history.

We can divide this again into four major stages:

1 GOD AND ISRAEL
God's mission through Israel

2 THE COMING OF JESUS
God's mission through Jesus

3 THE CHURCH
God's mission through the church

4 THE SECOND COMING
The completion of God's mission

This leads us into the final chapter of the biblical story – new creation. We will look at that in Unit 4.

In the rest of this unit we focus on God's mission through Israel.

THE FALL – WHAT WE LEARN

The Bible makes clear that the fall was a definite event in history, caused by sin. Sin spoils every aspect of God's creation:

Sin spoils every relationship
- Man's relationship with God
- Man's relationship with his fellow human beings
- Man's relationship with himself
- Man's relationship with the rest of creation

You can find examples of each of these in Genesis 3. Note them in the margin.

Sin spoils every dimension of human life
Look at Romans 1:18-32. List in the margin the different dimensions of life that are affected by sin.

Sin is universal
Sin affects the total personality, (Genesis 6:5). It affects all human beings (Romans 3:10–12:23). It affects the whole of human history. Genesis 4-11 describes the spread of sin from one generation to the next.

Sin affects both individual lives and corporate structures
This is because men and women are both individual and communal beings.

Where did sin come from? There is a mystery here. The Bible tells us that evil originated outside of mankind, but does not explain why God allowed it to enter his creation.

"Our concerns for pollution; our motivation to avert the ecological crisis; our anger at terrorism and our hatred of war; our delight in beauty and our support for the arts; our fighting against the depersonalizing trends of so much of modern ideology and for social and economic justice in the world; our longing to learn how to love our neighbours better – all these themes, which rightly fill the pages of much recent Christian writing, need all to be traced back to their beginnings. And their beginnings are to be found in the God who makes all things..."
David Atkinson, The Message of Genesis1-11

How odd of God to choose the Jews

"The story about the Tower of Babel concludes with God's judgement on mankind; there is no word of grace. The whole primeval history, therefore, seems to break off in shrill dissonance, and the question arises even more urgently: Is God's relationship to the nations now finally broken; is God's gracious forbearance now exhausted; has God rejected the nations in wrath forever?"
Gerhard von Rad,
Commentary on Genesis

MISSION THROUGH ISRAEL

Why the Jewish people?

From Genesis 12 onwards the Old Testament is the story of Israel. Why does this take up so much space? Why is the story of God's purpose so inextricably tied up with this one nation?

We get a clue from a passage like Isaiah 41:8-10:

*But you, Israel, my servant
Jacob, whom I have chosen,
the offspring of Abraham, my friend
you whom I took from the ends of
    the earth,
and called from its farthest corners,
saying to you, 'You are my servant,
I have chosen you and not cast you
    off';
be not dismayed, for I am your God;
I will uphold you with my victorious
    right hand.*

What does God call Israel (twice)?

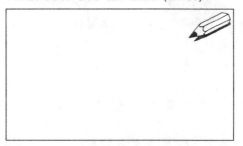

Who decided that Israel should be God's servant? What word does God use to indicate this?

Israel is called by God, chosen to be his servant. The initiative is his. God also reminds the nation of his sovereignty. He is the creator – 'the ends of the earth' belong to him.

What does it mean to be God's servant? Write your ideas here:

How did Israel become God's servant? We need to go back to the beginning. The passage refers to this when it calls Israel 'the offspring of Abraham, my friend'.

①

The pioneer servant

Genesis 12:1-3 tells us how Israel's servanthood began. This passage contains the foundation promise of the whole Bible. Turn to it now.
    What command does God give to Abraham?

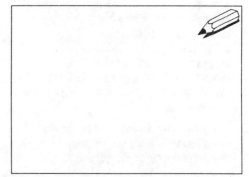

What are the three things he promises Abraham?

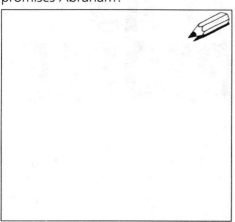

We need to see this in its context.

Genesis 1–11 gives us a breathtaking picture of God's world, created by him in all its beauty and splendour. Then come the disasters of the fall… the flood… Babel… Has God's plan failed?

Genesis 11:27–12:3 is a pivotal passage. The focus changes from the wide angle lens – the big picture – to zoom in on one family and then one individual.

Abraham is God's pioneer servant. He receives a command – Go – and three promises: the land which God will give; descendants who will be a great nation; and a blessing to all the nations or 'families' of the world.

There is a lot we could say about Abraham. From the story we pick out just two simple but important truths:

■ God still has a purpose for the whole world. His perspective is not limited by the seeming disasters to his creation.
■ And he uses people to fulfil his purpose…

This may seem obvious, but it is worth thinking about. God could have intervened directly to restore the damage, as he did at the flood. He could have worked through angels. But he chose to limit himself to working through his people.

This is a puzzle. Why did God identify himself so closely – exclusively – with Israel? Why does God insist on working through his church today? We are so imperfect, weak, uncertain… but this is God's mysterious purpose. He has chosen to work through his people rather than alone. He trusts us.

② The model community

Abraham is God's pioneer servant. An individual – often a lonely individual – he challenges us as individuals to demonstrate God's character in every walk of life and in every nation on earth.

But God's plan goes beyond individuals. Genesis 12:1–3 already speaks of Abraham's descendants and in 18:17–19 this is explicit. Abraham's children are to practise justice and righteousness and so fulfil God's purposes. Four hundred years later this was fulfilled as Israel became a nation in the drama of the Exodus.

Exodus 19:4–6 is another key passage. Look at it now.

God has brought the people miraculously out of Egypt. Now he claims them as his people, to belong to him – and to fulfil a special role.

What was God's purpose for his people? What were they to become? According to 19:6, they were to become…

> **a kingdom of priests…**

What God is saying is that the whole nation is to have a priestly character in relation to the other nations. It is to be the bridge or channel between God and the rest of the world. It is to show God's character to the world, and in some way to intercede (and suffer) on behalf of the world. God's people were also to become…

> **a holy nation**

The basic meaning of holiness is separation or difference. God is holy because he is absolutely different, absolutely separate from his creation. Human beings are called holy when they belong to him. Holiness means belonging to God and so being separate or different from others.

EXODUS 19

Exodus 19:4–6 shows the same pattern we have already seen in Isaiah 41:8–10:

■ God is sovereign over the world ('the whole earth is mine' verse 5). He has a universal purpose for his world.

■ God has chosen Israel. He has taken the initiative (verse 4) They belong to him (verse 5) in a special way.

■ God's choice has a purpose. There is a task for his people.

MEANWHILE…

For more about Abraham's particular role as God's servant, you can look at Part B, page 51.

LIVING AS GOD'S PEOPLE

LEVITICUS 19

Match this list of topics with the references below from Leviticus 19...

1. sacrifice and ritual
2. attitudes to the elderly
3. fair trading
4. worship of God
5. just and loving relationships
6. concern for the environment
7. sexual purity
8. occult practices
9. agriculture and generosity
10. concern for the weak and handicapped (which groups are mentioned?)

A. verses 3–4
B. verses 5–8
C. verses 9–10
D. verses 11,15–18
E. verses 13–14, 33–34
F. verses 3,32
G. verses 20–22,29
H. verses 23–25
I. verses 26–28,31
J. verses 35,36

Israel now belonged to God. He referred to her as 'my own possession' (verse 5), so she was to be different. She was to demonstrate God's character – not simply as a group of individuals, but as a whole society.

God's purpose is always both individual and corporate. The issues and problems of our world cannot be dealt with by individuals alone. Individual and community are not polarised in the Bible. They are different dimensions of what it is to be human.

And so God's purpose, beginning from Abraham, is to have *a community of people to be his servants.*

How did it work out?

Israel was to be a model community. How did this work out in practice? Immediately after calling Israel as his servant, God gave her his laws, through Moses. The laws of the Pentateuch spell out God's standards for all areas of life – from worship to economic affairs, family, social relationships, national life and politics, the order of society.

Leviticus 19 gives us a good idea of the extraordinary range of God's laws. Look at this chapter. What is the basis of God's command (verse 2)? Write your answer in the margin.

Now look at the top of the margin to see the areas that are covered by Leviticus 19.

The conclusion of the chapter seems almost an anti-climax. Fair weights and measures in the shops. Yet this last command is based on God's great deliverance from Egypt.

But...

What has all this got to do with mission? What do you think would be the effect, if Israel lived like this?

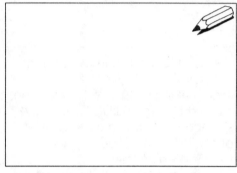

Deuteronomy 4:6–8 tells us what God intended for Israel. Other nations would see the difference and realise God's greatness.

What would be the impact on them, according to Deuteronomy 28:10?

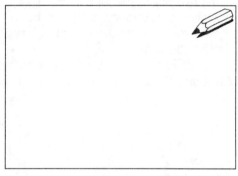

So Israel was to be a model community, a prototype of God's plan for the whole world. The other nations would be drawn to God through Israel.

This actually happened in the period between the Old and New Testaments, when the people of Israel were scattered and synagogues were planted throughout the Mediterranean world. Many Gentiles were drawn to the faith of the Jews, with its belief in One God, the Creator, and its clear ethical teaching. They were glad to turn from polytheism, with its idolatry and frequent lack of ethical standards.

This shows the power of the model to attract.

How does the church do this today? Should it be a model community?

If you are studying on your own, look at Activity C in the Group Activity section (page 49). Write down your reflections here.

❸
Failure and ideal

God's purpose was to be fulfilled through Israel his servant. But Israel failed. Totally, miserably, disastrously. Her history was one long story of disobedience.

Instead of being a model, distinct from the other nations, she had copied them. She had followed them into idolatry, injustice, immorality, oppression and violence. The prophets are full of descriptions of Israel's sin. The result was the judgment of the exile in Babylon.

Isaiah 40–55 reflects Israel's situation in exile. A key theme of these chapters is servanthood. We meet at least three servants here.

The disobedient servant

Israel is still God's servant. We started this study with God's words to her in Isaiah 41:8–10. But she was a failed servant.

Look at the description in Isaiah 42:18–22. What words are used to describe Israel?

What was the reason for Israel's situation (verse 24)? Write your answers in the margin.

Several other passages in these chapters reinforce the description of Israel's pathetic condition.

Can you think of parallels with the church? We have already thought about the church's failures (Unit 1) and of missionaries' failures (Unit 2) Can you think of any other examples, in your experience? Write in the margin.

We know all too well what it means to be the disobedient servant.

The secular servant

God's choice could turn next to Cyrus. We have a series of remarkable descriptions of this Persian King who rose to power and destroyed the corrupt Babylonian empire. He was a man of tolerance and openness, unique in his time. His rule brought religious freedom and the return of exiles to their homelands, including the people of Judah to Jerusalem.

Cyrus is described as God's instrument. God 'stirred him up' and brought him victory after victory (41:2–4:25). He foretold that he would rebuild the city of Jerusalem (44:28). Remarkably, God describes him as 'my shepherd' and 'anointed', the one who will 'fulfil all my purpose' (44:28–45:1). He grasps his 'right hand', surnames him and calls him (45:1–4). Cyrus is a key figure in God's plan. We could call him God's servant.

Yet Cyrus never acknowledged the true God. To him all the gods were the same and he acknowledged Yahweh to the Jews and Marduk to the Babylonians. He was a truly modern man!

Despite this God used him in a remarkable way. This reminds us of God's absolute control of what we call 'secular powers'. Not only are they under his control, but he can use them for his purpose, whether they acknowledge him or not.

But the secular power can never fulfil all God's purposes and so out of the failure of Israel, the disobedient servant, the focus changes.

We will look at the third of Isaiah's servants on the next pages.

TRUE OR FALSE?

What would you say are the implications of Leviticus 19 for Israel's understanding of her role? Mark the following statements True or False.

a) God wanted Israel to see that the whole of her life belonged to God.
b) God was more concerned with outward appearances than inner attitudes.
c) Israel's life as a society was meant to demonstrate God's ideal pattern.
d) God was concerned with the practical details of life as well as with true worship.

Check your answers at the foot of page 46 ➡

THE IDEAL SERVANT

Isaiah 42:1–9 introduces a new figure, unidentified, named simply 'my servant'. From his portrait we learn clearly what it means to be God's servant – the nature of his task and how it is carried out. This passage takes us to the heart of mission.

The servant's relationship to God

Look at Isaiah 42:1. What is the servant's relationship to God? Write your answer in the margin.

He is the one whom God has chosen, upholds, delights in (42:1). It is an intimate relationship, not like Cyrus, who did not respond, not even like any of the prophets before him. 'I have put my spirit upon him.' He has this relationship because of the presence of God's Spirit in a permanent way.

What is being stressed here once again is that to be a servant is to belong to God. The relationship is primary, not the task. The servant can fulfil his role because he belongs to God, not vice versa.

Think back to the list of qualities you would like to see in a missionary (Unit 2, page 32). What do you think is the most important quality for being involved in mission, in the light of this passage?

The servant's mission

The servant has a task. It is summarised in Isaiah 42:1 (the last line). What is it? Write your answer in the margin.

The content of his mission

In order to understand what this means, we need to look at the other references to his task in these verses:

■ justice is mentioned three times (verses 1, 3, 4)
■ his law (verse 4)
■ he will bring light (verse 6) and liberation (verse 7)

Try to summarise his mission in your own words, based on these references. Would you say it is more a mission of words, or of action? Write your answer in the margin.

What kind of mission is this? Is the servant a prophet? A teacher? Or is he a ruling figure, like Israel's kings who had administered justice? It seems that all three elements can be seen here. Behind him are the prophets, (often called 'my servants'); Moses 'the Lord's servant', prophet, law-giver and ruler. Behind him are also the kings, God's agents of justice. He sums up all these ministries.

So his task is to teach and proclaim God's truth. He has words to declare. But those words have power. They lead to action and liberation from injustice and error. There is no dichotomy.

Jesus perfectly exemplified this blend of word and action as he combined teaching and preaching with exorcism and healing.

His approach to mission

How does he approach his task? Look at verses 2–4. What are the seven things he will *not* do?

ANSWERS...

to the *True or False* questions on page 45: a) T, b) F, c) T, d) T

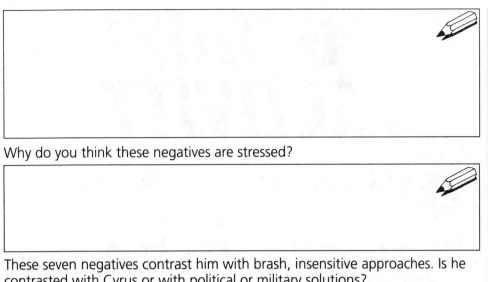

Why do you think these negatives are stressed?

These seven negatives contrast him with brash, insensitive approaches. Is he contrasted with Cyrus or with political or military solutions?

He does not reject or repudiate people. He perseveres until he wins them over. He will not fail himself, nor will he condemn others for their failure. Ultimately his mission will succeed.

The scope of his mission

How broad is his mission? Look at verses 1, 4 and 6.

The mission is to 'the nations' (verses 1, 6), 'the earth' and the 'coastlands' (verse 4). So the scope is universal. This is natural since God is the Creator of the whole world and all its people (verse 5). He is the only God (verse 8) to be worshipped by all. This reaffirms the scope of the original promise to Abraham. God's purpose has always been universal, never insular. His focus on Israel – apparently narrow – has always had this in view.

The urgency of his mission

'The coastlands wait for his law' (verse 4). The message of the servant is what people are waiting for, whether they realise it or not. Statistics remind us how many are still waiting. How long?

We can sum up the servant role in this diagram:

Abraham ➡ Israel ➡ Faithful Remnant ➡ **JESUS** ➡ 12 Disciples ➡ Church

God's choice begins with Israel (through Abraham). When Israel as a whole fails it is the faithful who continue. Jesus perfectly fulfils God's purpose. He is the ideal servant, the ideal Israel. He passes on the mandate through the apostles to the church.

The Old Testament looks forward

So we have traced God's purpose through the Old Testament. It begins from creation. It is threatened by the fall. But it continues through the people whom God calls his servants – both individuals and communities.

The Old Testament ends on a note of expectation, the longing for the ideal servant to come. We shall see in Unit 4 how Jesus fulfilled those longings – and transformed them.

Now look back and try to summarise in your own words Israel's role as God's servant, beginning from Abraham through to the ideal suffering servant.

THE SUFFERING SERVANT

Later passages develop the servant's task further. It becomes clear that God's purpose will involve suffering. In Isaiah 49:1–7 and 50:4–9 the servant affirms his commitment and confidence in God despite increasing pressure. The climax is the famous description of the suffering servant in Isaiah 52:13–53:12.

Who is this ideal, suffering servant?

Scholars have answered 'Yes' or 'No' to each of the following. What do you think?

■ Israel
■ Jesus
■ the church

In different ways the servant refers to them all. If you want to see some of the reasons, look at Part B (page 50)

WORKING ON YOUR OWN?

If you are working on your own, write your response to Activity A in the Group Activity section (page 48):

GROUP ACTIVITY

A. Who is God's servant today?

William Carey, a young shoemaker in Northampton, had a great desire to go to other countries and spread the gospel of God's redemptive grace. He founded the Baptist Missionary Society in 1792 and went to India the next year.

He was a great pioneer, the father of modern Protestant mission. But when he first presented his plans to his church, the elders told him:

> *Young man, if God wants to save the heathen, he will do it without any help from you or us.*

They believed so strongly in God's sovereignty that they did not think they had any responsibility. As you think about the story of God's dealings with Israel in history, what comment would you make? Would you agree with the elders? What would you say to them?

We have seen that Israel was 'called' to be God's servant. Whom does God 'call' today to be his servants? Christians have given different answers.

■ William Carey's elders probably would have said that God did not need any of us.
■ Others think that God's call is only to 'clergy' and full time workers'.
■ Some seem to think that God mostly calls women – especially to go to difficult places.

What do you think?

Bishop Azariah

Bishop Azariah was the first Indian Bishop in South India and leader of his church in a time of great mass movements to Christianity in the early part of this century.

He would tell each Christian whom he met in his diocese to put his hands on his head and say 'woe to me if I do not share the good news'. He told them that their baptism was their call to service and mission.

Was he right?

B. How wide is our mission?

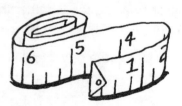

Our understanding of mission is based on the whole Bible. So we have been looking at the whole biblical story, beginning from creation and the fall.

Discuss your responses to the two case studies on pages 38 and 40.

If creation is the starting point, how wide is our mission…

■ geographically?
■ in the range of activities which we should include in mission?

Is there any limit? For example: which of these would you include in the church's mission? Which would you exclude? Why?

- concern for the environment
- voting in elections
- campaigning on social issues
- caring for the handicapped
- preaching over the radio or TV
- bringing up your family in a Christian way
- helping drug addicts
- worshipping together in small and large groups
- supporting trade unions
- writing books about the Christian faith and other faiths
- visiting neighbours
- taking exercise regularly

Please note: you may not be able to give a full answer to this yet. We will discuss it further in Units 4 and 5.

C. Making the model work

Israel was called to be a *model*, a prototype of God's purpose for the whole world.

How does this apply to the church today? We are not Israel – a theocratic state. Look at these three key passages.

■ 1 Peter 2:9–10

Peter is quoting directly from Exodus 19:4–6. Which phrases are taken from that passage?

What does Peter add, to explain the *purpose* of God's calling? (See the end of verse 9.)

What does this tell us about the church's role?

■ Matthew 5, 13–16

What do Jesus' vivid metaphors tell us about the church's role?

■ Ephesians 3:9–10

How do you think God's wisdom is to be 'made known' through the church? What does this tell us about the church's role?

Can you suggest practical examples from your situation?

Conclusion

God created this world for a purpose. He has not let go of it. But he is working out his purpose through his people. That includes us.

Pray for the church around the world, beginning with your area…

- that we will truly be God's servant
- that we will learn how to demonstrate God's character
- that we will each work out how to be an effective model in our own culture.

THE BIBLE FOR MISSION

In this part of the unit we look further at three areas that we began to discuss in Part A.

■ **Using the Bible for mission**
In Part A we looked at the Bible story as a whole. Why is this important? Read this page.

■ **God's servant in the Old Testament**
Our focus was on Israel, God's servant. Pages 51–52 look more closely at the role of Abraham and the suffering servant.

■ **Does the model work?**
There are tensions in trying to apply the example of Israel today. Read page 52.

There is no written assignment to be handed in for this unit. But you will find the material helpful for the assignments in Units 4 and 6.

Encountering the Bible

How should we use the Bible to understand more about mission? We expect everything to be instant these days:push in a card, press a few keys and out comes my ticket, or my cash, or the answer to my questions.

In one way the Bible's message is very simple. A young child can understand it. People have been converted by a single verse heard through a loudspeaker or picked up on a scrap of paper.

But the Bible is also a complex book – written by many people, over several hundred years, in different historical, geographical and social situations. It is a book from a different context. In order to let it speak to us accurately and completely, we need to understand it clearly in *its* context. At the same time, we must make sure that we apply it firmly to *our* context.

Holding these two contexts together requires some effort on our part, but it is well worth it.

Look at the box below. It lists four ways of making contact with the message of the Bible.

GETTING THE MESSAGE

Here are four simple suggestions for approaching the Bible to make sure that we really 'get the message' and experience its power.

1. Take in the broad sweep of the Bible story
Try to see the whole Bible as one story, beginning from creation right through to the completion of God's purpose in the book of Revelation. Seeing the whole story as one gives us an overall perspective.

2. Look for the historical development and the different perspectives of the writers
The Bible is one story, the story of mission, but it unfolds over hundreds of years and from different perspectives. For example, the psalmists wrestled with the problems of suffering and injustice. The only answer they found — perhaps the most important of all — was to leave the problems firmly in God's hands and keep turning back to him, not letting him go.

Job learned that suffering is not a sign of God's displeasure — it can be the opposite. Isaiah contributed the idea of suffering on behalf of others. It was only the coming of Jesus that showed the true meaning of suffering for others and the reality of victory over death.

We might say that we only need to know Jesus' answer to the problems. But as we enter into the struggles of earlier writers we learn further dimensions — and usually find that their struggles match our own.

Similarly we have four gospel pictures of Jesus, not one. Studied together, they give us a full three dimensional (four dimensional?) figure, not a flat drawing. Paul and James give two perspectives on the relationship between faith and works. And so on.

3. Let the Bible speak to the issues and questions of our day
We don't read the Bible just as an ancient text. We bring to it questions from our context, our daily life. How do I resolve the personal ethical difficulties I face: the pressure to conform, to be competitive, the problem of relationships. What does the Bible say to the issues of society: the environment, the nuclear threat, poverty and affluence, our pluralistic culture with so many different faiths and world views?

We bring our questions to the Bible, but we also let the Bible question us. What about my attitude to material possessions? Why do I think it is unfair that God should judge people? Is my thinking about culture biblical or just western?

4. Bring together the Bible's teaching on major truths
What does the Bible teach us about God? About the world in which we live — its origin and destiny? What does the Bible teach us about humanity — our potential and value as well as our fatal flaws? What is our problem and how do we overcome it? Is there a Saviour or do we have resources already within us? Where does it all lead to? What is the ultimate purpose of life?

How does the Bible's teaching compare with that of other faiths and world views? Are they similar on some points? Incompatible with others? This kind of comparison helps us understand and appreciate our faith more.

Sometimes we want to jump straight to these questions. But we need to go through the other stages first. They will keep us from superficial or misleading answers. In these two units we can only attempt the first stage. We have tried to take in the broad sweep of the biblical story — the story of mission.

GOD'S SERVANT

On pages 42–48 we looked first at Abraham and then at the concept of God's servant. Let's take these in turn.

What did God want Abraham to do? Two things stand out in Genesis 12 and the following chapters. They are rather a surprise.

Going

'Go… so Abraham went, as the Lord had told him.' Abraham was to go physically, to leave his own country, relatives, even his immediate family – all the things that were important to him. (As an eastern son, he would normally have lived in his father's household until he died.)

God has always called some of his servants to do the same, to leave country or family, career or marriage, to cross geographical or cultural barriers. For the past 200 years the majority have been from a European or North American background.

Today there are increasing numbers from Africa, Asia, Latin America and the Pacific. God's servants come from all continents to all continents.

Being

What did Abraham do once he had gone? It is not obvious at first sight. He appears to have lived the normal life of a wealthy clan leader, moving with his household, cattle and flocks.

In Genesis 14 we are told that Abraham could muster 318 fighting men, so there must have been at least 600–700 adults altogether in his group.

He did not preach or evangelise. There is only one recorded incident when he mentioned the name of Yahweh to outsiders – the king of Sodom in Genesis 14.

The focus of the narrative is more on how Abraham lived than on what he said or achieved. His being was more important than his doing. God was concerned with his way of life and the attitudes on which these were based. Once again, we need to see this in context. What kind of life were people living in his time? What were the issues and problems of his day?

The early chapters of Genesis reveal a stark picture. In this context, what was Abraham's role? To live differently as God's servant, demonstrating the reality and character of God. Several characteristics stand out in Abraham's life.

- worship
- dependence on God
- receiving God's forgiveness
- intercession
- standing for justice

We can sum it up in the word *demonstrating*. Abraham is the pioneer servant, living in a society which does not know the true God, demonstrating by his presence the reality of God; witnessing by his different life to the character of God.

Turning now to the Old Testament picture of God's servant, we can ask, 'Who is the Suffering Servant?'

There are three major answers to this question.

1. Israel: God's people

We have focused in this study on Israel as God's servant. We have seen God's plan for a model community, beginning from Abraham. Israel was God's servant as a whole nation, called to be priestly and holy, a light to the nations. Within Israel there were also great figures (Moses, the Prophets, the Kings) who specially fulfilled the servant role.

FURTHER READING

Two books which spell out the Bible story as a whole and relate it to mission.
God's Mission: Healing the Nations, David Burnett, MARC Europe.
Mission to Man in the Bible, Roger Hedlund, Evangelical Literature Service, Madras.

Also...

Culture to Culture, the open learning course in mission, goes right through the four stages we have listed, and more. See Unit 8 for details.

Ripening Harvest, Gathering Storm has a good section called 'The Master Plan of the Servant' (pp.23–40). It summarises the biblical material well.

DOES THE MODEL WORK?

We saw how Israel's example was effective, especially in the period between the Old and New Testaments, when Israel was scattered among the nations. Gentiles were attracted by what they saw (page 44).

This shows us the importance of Israel actually going *out* to where people were, rather than just waiting for them to come to her. (Of course, Israel did not choose to go out; she was forced by her situation.)

The culture tension

But there was also a tension in the concept of the model.

Some of those gentiles actually became Jews, undergoing circumcision and submitting to the whole law in all its details. They were called proselytes. Others could not go so far. The detailed demands were too much for them, especially the rigid dietary and social regulations. They would cut them off from their relatives and society. So they remained on the fringe and were called 'God-fearers'.

(Many of the early gentile Christians were from these two groups. They were very ready for the gospel when it came to them).

Think back to our discussion of culture (Unit 2, page 27, margin). We saw that the gospel affects all of life. Our study of Israel as a *model* community reinforces this.

But we can also see the problem: how do you relate the model to each person's culture? Do all have to become 'Jews', adopting Jewish culture and laws, like the proselytes? Is there a 'standard' Christian model into which all converts have to fit?

How do we help churches to work out their own 'model' for their situation? We shall return to this again in Units 4 and 5.

Israel certainly suffered – supremely in the punishment of the exile – but also from the beginning of her history in Egypt. She was a small, insignificant nation, constantly buffeted and squeezed between the great powers. Israel did serve as a light to the surrounding nations. Her ways were different, as acknowledged by the kings of Syria, Naaman's conversion and similar incidents in her history.

But Israel failed, disastrously. She was not sinless. Much of her suffering was punishment.

So what is said about the servant in these chapters must go beyond Israel – in fact far beyond Israel.

And yet Israel was (and is still) God's people. God continued to involve her in his purpose for the world. Some of her suffering was for God's sake (see Psalm 44:22). Some at least were faithful – the remnant within Israel.

So there was still a reference to Israel in these chapters. But the servant cannot be Israel alone.

2. Jesus: The perfect fulfilment

Jesus saw himself as God's servant, fulfilling the role described here. He quoted from Isaiah 53:12 when he described himself as the servant who gives 'his life as a ransom for many' (Mark 10:4–5; see Luke 22:27). He said that his blood was to be poured out 'for many' (Mark 14:24) and that he was to be 'numbered among the transgressors' (Luke 22:37).

At Jesus's baptism and transfiguration, the voice from heaven described him as the 'beloved… with whom I am well pleased' (Matthew 3:17; 17:5), words from Isaiah 42:1. Matthew quotes Isaiah 53:4 (Matthew 8:17) and 42:1–4 (Matthew 12:15–21) to explain Jesus' ministry. John quotes Isaiah 53:1 to explain the unbelief of the Jews.

The Book of Acts shows that the earliest preaching of the apostles identified Jesus as God's servant (Acts 3:13, 26; 4:27, 30) – the Greek word *pais* literally means 'boy' or 'lad', and hence servant. We have the famous incident of the Ethiopian eunuch reading Isaiah 53 and asking

---

Philip to explain it. 'And beginning from the Scripture he told him the good news of Jesus' (Acts 8:30–35).

There are other echoes in the New Testament, but these are enough to make quite clear that Jesus perfectly fulfilled the description of these passages. We are looking at his suffering for our sins.

3. The church: the servant community

But it is striking that the New Testament writers do not stop by identifying the servant with Jesus.

Paul quotes Isaiah 49:6 in his preaching at Antioch of Pisidia (Acts 13:47ff). but he applies it to himself and Barnabas, preaching the gospel to the gentiles. The servant was to be a light to the nations – 'we are fulfilling that role by our preaching' says Paul.

In 2 Timothy 2:24 he quotes Isaiah 42:2ff: 'the servant of the Lord must not be quarrelsome…', applying it to any Christian worker. Romans 8:33ff is the magnificent passage of confidence: 'Who shall bring any charge against God's elect?… who is to condemn?' He is echoing Isaiah 50:8ff in the context of facing suffering and opposition. So the church takes up the servant role.

Israel – the prophets – Jesus – the apostles – the church – which is the servant? The answer is that all of them are because all of them represent God's people, who are his servants, collectively and individually.

THE
WORLD
CHRISTIAN
Unit 4

THE UPSIDE-DOWN KINGDOM

CONTENTS

PURPOSE

PART A   The purpose of this unit is to help you to understand the impact of the Kingdom of God in the New Testament, in the life and teaching of Jesus and the life of the early church. You will also describe Paul's strategy and theology of mission and explain what the final part of the biblical story tells us about mission.

PART B   You will make a summary of the biblical story of mission and prepare to present it to your church or group.

UNEXPECTED KING

The story so far

The Bible is a story, the story of mission. We have summed it up in four events. Can you remember them? Look back at page 37 if you need to. How far along the story does the Old Testament take us? How many of those events does it include? Can you summarise its story in 3–4 lines: (the essence of what we looked at in Unit 3)?

We now continue Stage 3 of the biblical story

Redemption in history

Israel had failed. She was sent into exile and was no longer a nation. The Old Testament closes with a few people back in Jerusalem and the rebuilding of the Temple. But there was no restoration of the kingdom, no return to the glories of David.

God's purpose, revealed by the prophets, had narrowed down first to the remnant of Israel, then to an individual who would be his ideal servant.

In the 400 years between the Old and New Testaments expectations sometimes flared up to fever pitch, then faded away in the drudgery of everyday life under occupation, first by Greeks, then by Romans. But the expectations were always there, focused now on *Messiah*, the anointed one who would supremely represent God's interest and usher in his Kingdom.

And then he came. The revolutionary preacher from Nazareth stirred people up with his healings and exorcisms. His fresh spontaneous preaching made God seem very near, a loving Father rather than the distant emperor of current Jewish thinking. Crowds flocked to him. People stampeded to get near him. Surely this was the one who would bring back the Kingdom?

The Messiah who didn't fit

And yet … he did not fit their expectations. The conventional interpretations of Scripture were not being fulfilled. There was no royal splendour of a new King David. There was no call to the nation to revive its former glories, to rise up under God and unite against its oppressors.

He appeared to brush aside the title of Messiah – not rejecting it so much as ignoring it, preferring the enigmatic and anonymous 'Son of Man'. Only the most careful student of Scripture could see that Jesus was in fact closely following the *servant* model of Isaiah, patiently teaching, siding with the most unlikely people,

IN SUMMARY

God created the world for his own purpose and gave it to men and women to be his stewards and agents (Creation). But they sinned and fell and spoiled God's creation (Fall). God called Abraham and through him he planned a people, Israel, to be his servant. They were to be a model community, a prototype of God's purpose for the whole world, demonstrating his character, radiating light and truth (Redemption in History: Israel).

3 TENSIONS

We have already noticed some tensions in the story so far:

 How wide is mission?
It begins from creation, so it is very broad and wide. But are there any limits? What about the effects of the fall?

You may have tried to answer that in the previous Unit (page 48) but you probably found it quite difficult, because the story so far is not complete. There are some more things we need to know: How did Jesus and the apostles look at the world? What is God's ultimate purpose for his world? That may help us to clarify the goal of mission and so decide how wide it should be.

② Israel was to be a model society.
But to join it you had to become a Jew, leaving your own culture behind. Could this model cross cultural barriers? Was it limited to one culture, or could it be adapted to fit into any culture? Was God's purpose the expansion of the nation Israel?

③ Israel failed.
Not just once, but repeatedly. How could God's purpose be carried out by fallible human beings? Was his way only open to the 'good', the 'righteous' and 'religious'? Is it only those who keep God's law who can be his servants?

These are three basic questions which we need to answer in order to have a mission that works for our world today. Watch out for some answers in this Unit.

---

avoiding media ballyhoo and hype, and resisting evil and injustice (Matthew 12:18–20).

The result was inevitable: a clash with the authorities, arrest, summary trial, and execution. It was all over in less than three years.

Or rather it had just begun. The drama of the resurrection was followed by the explosion of Pentecost, creating the movement that is still gathering momentum today.

What kind of Kingdom?

What was the centre of Jesus' life and ministry? What was new and different? The Kingdom of God was at the centre of his teaching. But what kind of Kingdom? Clearly it meant different things to different people.

Jesus fulfilled the Old Testament expectations. The only problem was that his contemporaries failed to understand.

They read the scriptures from their own context of oppression and humiliation by the Romans. They read them from the perspective of wounded national pride and self-righteousness. So they were looking for liberation in their terms, nationalistic and ritualistic, preserving the monopoly and privilege of the religious leaders, preserving the exclusive position of Israel as the nation next to God.

Some of them rejected this. They opposed the hierarchy of their day. Their response was to withdraw, some into the desert like the Essenes of the Dead Sea community. They waited for the triumph of good over evil in apocalyptic and cataclysmic events – great battles, supernatural intervention, and the restoration of the people of God, the 'sons of light' against the 'sons of darkness'.

Others had given up waiting for God and turned to the skill of their own brains and right arms. They believed that only violent revolution would get rid of the Romans and they were willing to pay the price.

And of course some had come to terms with the situation, settling down and making what they could out of the occupation. They were more interested in material benefits here and now. They did not mind whether they gained them from the oppressors or from their own people, or preferably both.

A few set out to live the life of faith as best they could, looking for God's help and waiting for his intervention in his way.

Does all this sound familiar? Think of the different ways in which people today respond to the problems of our world and the solutions they are looking for. There are plenty of parallels between the first and the twentieth centuries.

MATTHEW, MARK, LUKE...

The Synoptic Gospels refer most to the Kingdom of God ('Kingdom of heaven' in Matthew). John mentions the Kingdom but refers more to 'eternal life'.

UPSIDE-DOWN KINGDOM

Here are some of the things Jesus had to say about God's Kingdom...

> May your kingdom come, may your will be done on earth as it is in heaven.

> The kingdom of God is within you.

> The kingdom of God is near! Turn away from your sins and believe the Good News!

> My kingdom does not belong to this world.

> Your Father is pleased to give you the kingdom.

So what was Jesus' message of the Kingdom? We need to look at the Gospels.

The Kingdom is present here and now

Read Mark 1:15 (or Matthew 4:17). What does it say about the Kingdom? Use the margin to make notes.

John the Baptist had the same message (Matthew 3:2), but Jesus seems to have gone a step further than John. Look at Matthew 12:28 and Luke 17:20–21. Where is the Kingdom? Note your answer in the margin.

Some interpret Jesus' words in Luke as meaning that the Kingdom is something 'in you' – it is internal, or even mystical. But it seems better to translate it 'the Kingdom is among you'. (Nowhere else in the synoptic Gospels is the Kingdom within people; it is near us and we enter it). It is already here, in the presence of Jesus.

The Kingdom is visible

Jesus told his disciples that they were very privileged people. Look at Matthew 13:16–17 and Luke 10:23.

What was their privilege? Use the margin to make notes.

They were seeing things that others had longed to see. People had waited centuries for this day.

What were they seeing? Read Luke 7:18–23 and write down some of the things which they saw:

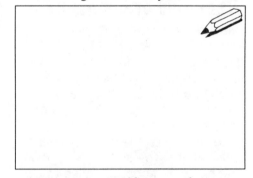

What was the significance of Jesus' preaching and miracles ? When we look at the question which John the Baptist's disciples brought to Jesus, it is evident that Jesus wanted them to realise that these were *signs* of who he was. He was 'the one who is to come', the agent of God's Kingdom. John's gospel always refers to Jesus miracles as 'signs' (John 2:11). They were intended to show people who he was.

It was not only preaching and healing. Look at Matthew 12:27–29. What else did Jesus do and what was

56 UNIT 4

this a sign of? Use the margin to make notes.

When Jesus cast out demons this was the sign that the Kingdom had come. He told his disciples that he had seen Satan defeated when they told him how they had cast out demons (Luke 10:17–18).

So the Kingdom was not something invisible and 'spiritual'. It could be seen. It was demonstrated in Jesus' works *and* words. Notice how these are never separated.

Look at Matthew 9:35 and Luke 4:18–19. Make a list of Jesus' activities, the signs of the Kingdom.

The Kingdom is for outcasts

Jesus set the tone for his ministry when he went to Matthew's party. Read Mark 2:15–17. What did Jesus say in answer to his critics? Use the margin to make notes.

Now look at the following stories. Why would the people in them have been considered outcasts in Jesus' time? And what was Jesus' attitude to them?

Mark 5:25–34

Luke 19:1–10

Luke 7:37–39, 44–50

Luke 10:39–42

John 4:7–9, 25–27, 34

Mark 1:40–42

Matthew 8:5–11

Matthew 15:21–28

Luke 10:33

John 12:22

This was hard to take. The religious leaders did not like this at all (for example, see Mark 2:16; 12:12).

And Jesus could be quite provocative too. Look at his behaviour when invited to dinner in the Pharisee's house (Luke 14:1):

■ verses 7–11: his advice to people who liked to be in the best seats…
■ verses 12–14: he tells his host who to invite next time…

■ One of the guests chimed in piously with a reference to the Kingdom of God (verse 15). But Jesus told a story about what the Kingdom is really like. Look at the people who were to be the guests (verse 21) – the poor, the maimed, the blind and the lame. And look what happened to those who were originally invited (verse 24).

JESUS & THE YUPPIE

The rich young ruler also found Jesus demanding (Mark 10:17–22). Jesus loved him but had to give him some hard conditions, which proved too much. Notice how the disciples responded when Jesus told them that this was the problem for rich people. 'Who can be saved?' they asked (10:26). They believed that riches were a sign of God's blessing. But Jesus was turning their values upside-down.

The disciples were slow to learn. Look at the story of James and John which follows immediately (Mark 10:35–45). The other disciples were furious because they had not got their claim in sooner! See how Jesus taught them.

STEPS IN JESUS' MISSION

Some people have been puzzled at Jesus' attitude to the Syro-Phoenician woman (Matthew 15:21–28). It is evident that Jesus was testing her to see whether she was genuine. We can also see that Jesus was following a definite order in his mission.

In Matthew 28:18–20 he ordered his disciples to go to *all nations*. That was the ultimate goal (remember God's promise to Abraham in Genesis 12). But first he must minister to Israel (Matthew 15:24; see also Matthew 10:5 and 6:23). And before he could reach Israel he first had to call his 12 disciples, with whom he spent the most time.

THE KING'S AUTHORITY

Look at these passages and match them with the examples of authority:

1. Mark 2:10
2. Matthew 7:21–23
3. Matthew 5:17
4. Matthew 25:31–46
5. Luke 4:21

A. Power to turn people away from their eternal destiny
B. Authority to fulfil the law
C. The King: people are responding to him when they serve others
D. Scripture finds its fulfilment in him
E. Authority both to forgive sins and to heal

The Kingdom involves suffering

Look at Matthew 8:20; Mark 8:31; 9:31; 10:33; 10:45; 14:36. What was the cost for Jesus?

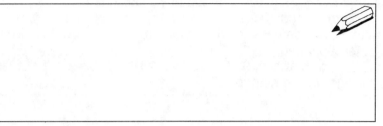

What will be the cost for his followers?: Look at Matthew 5:10–12; Mark 9:34; Luke 14:26, 27, 33; Mark 10:21, 29–30. (Compare this with Paul's comment in Acts 14:22.)

Jesus is at the centre of the Kingdom

At the centre of all this activity, this astonishing reversal of values, is a person.
   He has tremendous authority. Look at the material in the margin.
   But the overwhelming impression is one of grace, forgiveness, acceptance. That is why the outcasts come to him. And that is why the Kingdom is accessible, because there is a person to whom we can respond.
   What was Jesus' basic command to people whom he met? (See for example Mark 1:17; 2:14; 3:13; 8:34–35; 10:21.)

Look at John 1:12; 3:16. What do people need to do in order to enter God's family?

The Kingdom of God is not a set of principles, or a code of ethics, but a person.
   (This became much clearer to the early church after the resurrection and ascension of Jesus. They could focus on him as their Lord, reigning in heaven but present with them by his Spirit. That was later, but even in his earthly lifetime the Gospels show us this focus on a person).

The Kingdom is not yet complete

In Acts 1:6, the disciples are still expecting the coming of the Kingdom.
   There is no doubt that the Kingdom has already come, but Jesus also points out that it is not complete.

Look at his parables about seeds (Mark 4:27; Matthew 13:24–30, 39–43) What do they tell us about the Kingdom?

[pencil icon]

There is a process of growth. It is not yet complete. He refers to 'the close of the age', which has not yet come.

The Son of Man has come as a lowly figure, but what will he be in the future? (See Mark 8:38; 9:1; 14:62.)

[pencil icon]

He will come again in power and glory. Jesus refers back to Daniel 7:13–14, the vision of God's final intervention. It has still not happened yet.

In the meantime, the gospel is to be preached (Matthew 24:14). Then the end will come.

The upside-down Kingdom

So this is the upside-down Kingdom. It is quite different from what anybody had expected.

What do you find surprising or striking? Write your comments here. Think also of the three questions we raised at the beginning of the unit (page 55). What answers do you find so far?

[pencil icon]

Jesus' teaching on the Kingdom is very relevant to our three questions.
■ How wide is mission? Jesus deals with the whole person. The Kingdom affects the physical, moral, social and spiritual dimensions of life.
■ What about cultural barriers? They are still there – Jesus' ministry is first to Israel – but beginning to be broken down. The Kingdom reaches beyond the 'regular' society of Israel.
■ What about failure? Evidently Jesus accepted and forgave. People who felt they were failures were quite at ease with him – while the self-righteous and self-sufficient were excluded. People could respond to the *person* of Jesus, and so were drawn into God's Kingdom. They could acknowledge the King.

So Jesus' upside-down Kingdom draws people in. It is relevant to mission – then and now.

How did it work out in practice after Jesus? How did the Kingdom become real to people?

We turn from the Gospels to the book of Acts.

THE KINGDOM COMMUNITY

These passages from the Book of Acts give us vivid pictures of the early church and its life. Match them with the community characteristics listed below. After each passage, list the letters indicating the characteristics found in it.

Add any others that you find which are not listed.

1. Acts 2:42–47
2. 4:31–35
3. 5:11–16
4. 6:40–41
5. 8:1–4

A. care for the needy
B. apostolic teaching
C. worship and praise of God
D. growth in numbers
E. prayer
F. the power of the Holy Spirit
G. signs and wonders by the apostles
H. fellowship and common life
I. suffering
J. impact on society
K. apostolic witness and preaching
L. holiness of life; judgement on sin
M. people being saved
N. witness by all members

Compare these characteristics with Jesus' teaching about the Kingdom. What do you find the same? Are there any differences?

The servant community

Jesus ascended. but his ministry of the Kingdom continued. Look at the early verses of Acts 1. Luke tells us that his earlier narrative (in the Gospel of Luke) was the *beginning* of Jesus' actions and words (Luke 1:1). Now they continue.

The disciples were waiting for the Kingdom. Jesus spoke about it to them (1:3, 6).

It is important to remind ourselves that Jesus had spent time with certain people in his ministry. Not just any people, but a select and key group – the 12 who were the inner circle, and also the larger group of disciples.

Why did Jesus choose *12* disciples?

It was not an accident: it was the number of the tribes of Israel. Jesus was beginning to rebuild Israel – the Israel that had failed so often in the past.

In Acts 1 it was this group that gathered together, along with a larger number. The day of Pentecost came, with the explosive power of the Holy Spirit. The group of disciples were transformed into a new and dynamic community.

Think back to the diagram in Unit 3. Fill in the right hand side below (check page 47 if you need to).

So the church is the continuation of God's purpose for his servant. It is the *servant community*.

What does this mean?

Look at Acts 13:47. Paul is quoting Isaiah 49:6. To whom were these words originally spoken? To whom does Paul apply them in his day?

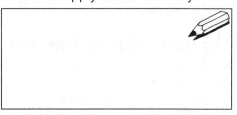

God's purpose for his servant in the Old Testament is being fulfilled now, through the apostles, through the church. They are the servant community.

So God's Kingdom is being expressed and established through the community of his people. (We looked at 1 Peter 2:9–10 in Unit 3 (page 49). It also speaks of the church as Israel, God's servant).

*Note: We are not saying here that the church **is** the Kingdom. We shall see later how Kingdom and church relate to each other (pages 64–65).*

What kind of community is this? What are its characteristics? Look at the passages in the margin. They give us vivid pictures of the early church and its life.

The characteristics of the early church are very much the characteristics of the Kingdom of God, as Jesus taught and demonstrated (see the margin). But certain aspects have now been developed and made explicit, such as:

■ the power and presence of the Holy

Abraham ➡ Israel ➡ Faithful Remnant ➡ **JESUS** ➡   ➡

Spirit in a new way. This is the key to the early church's life and mission.
■ the community life and fellowship of the early church.
■ baptism and the breaking of bread (the Lord's Supper)
■ the increasing numbers

As we have already noticed (pages 58–59), their focus was on Jesus, the King, now reigning as Lord. They were not looking for a national kingdom, or earthly territory. 'Jesus is Lord' became a key summary of their beliefs.

What about cultural barriers?

So the new community grew in Acts. Of course, there were problems and crises. Several are described in Acts. Perhaps the biggest was the question of culture.

The first Christians were all Jews. They naturally saw themselves as the true Israel, the fulfilment of God's servant purpose. So they assumed that to follow Jesus, the Jewish Messiah, one would need to become a Jew. In fact, they did not see themselves as distinct from the Jewish faith. They were the true Jews.

So what about Gentiles? At first they did not really think about them.

Look at Acts 11:19. To whom did they preach about Jesus?

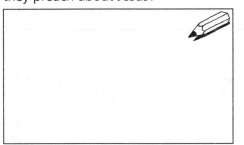

God had to intervene directly, and rather dramatically, to jolt Peter into realising God's attitude to the Gentiles. Look at the story of Cornelius in Acts 10 (see especially verses 18ff and 34ff).

The incident caused a sensation. Not everybody was pleased (11:1–3). But Peter's explanation of his vision silenced his critics and people apparently accepted that Gentiles could be baptised in the name of Jesus and receive the Holy Spirit (11:18).

When Cornelius responded to the preaching in Antioch, the church leaders sent Barnabas to investigate (Acts 11:20–22). His open attitude encouraged more growth and the church made enough impact on society to get itself a new name (11:23–26). They were no longer just Jews.

The Jerusalem Council

Paul and Barnabas' missionary journey brought many more Gentile converts and then came the reaction:

What were these converts? Were they part of God's people? If so, did they not have to become Jews?

The question split the church. Look at Acts 15:1–2 and Galatians 2:11–14. What was Paul's view? Whom did he have to oppose? Do you think it was easy?

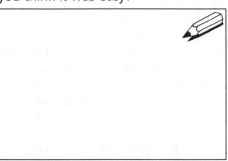

The problem was so difficult and divisive that a special meeting was called. Acts 15 describes the Council of Jerusalem – the first great council of the church.

Look at their conclusions (15:19–21, 28–29). What was their answer to the question of culture? Do you think they solved it?

The Council was decisive. The Jewish cultural requirements were not binding on converts. But some standards, based on the Old Testament, were set to guide them in working out their faith from their own cultural background.

THINK ABOUT IT...

■ The issue of culture was resolved in principle. But in practice it remained, and still remains. How do you develop a *Christian* culture? Is there such a thing? What actions and customs are compatible and what are incompatible?

■ The Kingdom is concerned with inner attitudes rather than external things, which can be secondary. But this still needs to be worked out in each context and culture.

Can you think of cultural practices on which Christians are divided today?

WORKING ON YOUR OWN?

If you are studying on your own, look at Activities A and B of the Group Activities (page 67). Write your response now.

PAUL THE AMBASSADOR

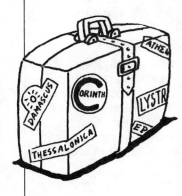

Luke introduces Paul as the great ambassador of the Kingdom, the ideal apostle or missionary. He is not the only one, of course, but from Luke and from Paul's letters we know more about his strategy and theology than about any other apostle. We shall look very briefly at these.

Paul's strategy

Here are three obvious but fundamental things that we learn from Paul. (There are many other things that could be said).

■ **We have to take the gospel to people where they are** This is not as obvious as it seems. The early Christians did not leave Jerusalem. Only persecution scattered them (Acts 8:1, 4; 11:19). What happened in Acts 13 was something new.

In the Old Testament, Israel was to be a model. People would come to her. They would worship at Jerusalem (see for example Isaiah 2:2, 3). But now God's people are to *go out* to every part of the world.

Paul's strategy was apparently to go to the major cities and population centres, for example Ephesus (Acts 19). As a result the word would be spread throughout a region (see Acts 19:10).

In another sense also, Paul went to people 'where they are'. He tried to present the gospel in their thought forms. Look at Acts 17:22–31. How did Paul approach the Athenians? (We shall look at this passage again in unit 5.)

■ **The local church is the key to mission** Paul established churches and left them to look after themselves. Look at Acts 14:21–23. Compare this with Acts 20:17, 28, 32.

■ Who were the leaders of the local churches?

■ What was their responsibility?

■ To whom or what did Paul commit them for their continued growth and development?

Of course, Paul did not leave these new churches completely alone. He visited them, prayed for them, wrote letters. They were constantly on his heart (2 Corinthians 11:28). But they were the essential 'units', the basic groups of God's people in their area. They were responsible to live as God's people and were to demonstrate God's character and purpose in their place.

See, for example, 1 Thessalonians 1:8; Philippians 1:27.

So mission was not just the task of a few people, the apostles, or the missionaries, or the Jerusalem Christians. It was the privilege and responsibility of each local church. Not on their own – there were apostles and prophets and teachers and others who travelled, to encourage and build up the churches and to plant new ones.

Paul himself wanted to be a partner with the churches in spreading the gospel. He thanked them for their encouragement and invited them to share with him in his apostolic ministry.

If you want to study this further look at Part B, (pages 69 and 70).

■ **The gospel is for people of all cultures** Paul was passionately committed to this, as we have already seen (Acts 15 and Galatians 2). He consciously sought to adapt his presentation of the good news to each person's culture.

See 1 Corinthians 9:19–23.

Can you think of examples of this today? Do you know situations where this kind of adaptation is needed? Or examples of people successfully adapting to another culture?

(We will look at this again in Unit 5.)

Paul's theology

Paul's theology is consciously related to the question of culture. How can God's Kingdom be truly universal, so that it is accessible to people of all cultures?

Even more fundamental, how can the Kingdom be truly accessible to people of all backgrounds, whatever their religious status, whatever their failures?

These are two of the fundamental questions we asked at the beginning of the unit. Paul finds the answer to both in the gospel of God's grace.

In his letter to the Romans he wrestles with these questions. Romans 1:16 is the basic statement: the gospel is 'the power of God' to save *all* people.

But how? Look at Romans 3:20–26. How do you think the gospel is able to save *all* people?

Essentially this is because it is by grace, received through faith. It does not depend on *any* human achievement (Romans 3:22–24), because all human efforts and achievements fall short of God's absolute standards. (3:20,23). God has provided the solution himself in the death and resurrection of Jesus (3:25; 4:25).

This radical understanding of the gospel sets it free to fit into any culture. It is not just for Jews. It also means that it is good news to people of all religious backgrounds, or no religious background. It is truly universal.

The rest of Romans works this out in detail. We do not have space to study this vast theme any further here. But it is vital for us to realise that this gospel is for *all*.

(See Unit 5 for the whole question of the uniqueness and universality of the gospel).

Romans 14 and 1 Corinthians 8–10 show that there were continuing differences among Christians of different backgrounds. What are the two issues mentioned in Romans 14:1, 5?

Paul offers several approaches to resolve the differences. Notice his reference to the Kingdom of God in 14:17. What does this tell us about the relationship between the Kingdom and culture?

CHURCH, KINGDOM, WORLD

If the Kingdom was the centre of Jesus' teaching, then what about the church? Did it replace the Kingdom? What is the relationship between the church and the Kingdom? And how do they both relate to the world?

Christians have given at least three major answers:

1. The church *is* the Kingdom of God

Some Christians have identified the church with the Kingdom of God. This can lead to two opposite results:

■ Either the church seeks to dominate the world...

If the church and God's Kingdom are identical then the extension of God's Kingdom means the extension of the power and influence of the church. The 'Holy Roman Empire' was the symbol of one effort to see all powers under God's authority. But it led to severe distortions.(This tendency was seen at its worst in the attempts of medieval popes to dominate European politics).

■ Or the church withdraws from the world.

If all God's activity is confined to the church, then the church can afford to lose interest in the world and concentrate on the 'spiritual'. The world is merely a staging post for heaven. This kind of withdrawal is sometimes called 'pietism'. Some politicians today want the church to stay out of anything 'temporal', like political or economic issues.

2. The kingdom of God is entirely separate from the church

Some Christians stress God's work in the world quite apart from the church. The 'people of God' is the whole human community. God's activity in the world is seen in anything which brings justice and compassion, or physical, social, political change. This perspective rightly emphasises God's activity in the world. But it can lead to an over-emphasis on social and political action. From this perspective, Chairman Mao of China was seen as a 'Saviour', God's agent of salvation.

3. The church is the sign and agent of the Kingdom

The church is not the same as the Kingdom of God, because God's work is greater than the church. But it is not separate from it. The church is the *sign* of the Kingdom. Its members are the people of the Kingdom; God's agents in the world.

All the world belongs to God, because he is King. He can and does work through anybody whom he chooses, even if they do not acknowledge him. But the church is the community of those that acknowledge him as King and seek to live their lives by the principles of his Kingdom. They want to extend his rule to all areas of life, so that ultimately all will acknowledge him.

In this perspective, the church, the Kingdom and the world are seen as concentric circles.

Which of these answers do you think is the most helpful and biblical?

CHURCH & KINGDOM

WORLD

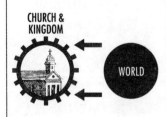

CHURCH & KINGDOM

WORLD

KINGDOM at work in the WORLD

CHURCH

CHURCH

KINGDOM

WORLD

The end of the story: new creation

If the world belongs to God, where is it going? What is the ultimate goal of mission? We come to the last stage in the biblical story.

When Jesus came, he inaugurated the Kingdom. It was decisive. From then on his followers are living in the last age (Hebrews 1:2; 1 Corinthians 10:11). We are already part of his Kingdom (Colossians 1:13). We have tasted the powers of the age to come (Hebrews 6:5).

But as we saw earlier, even Jesus taught that the Kingdom has not yet fully come. Paul reminds us that we are still living in 'this present evil age' (Galatians 1:4). We are still waiting.

Romans 8:18–25 is perhaps his most famous and moving description of this waiting. Look at it now:

■ Who or what is waiting?

■ What are they waiting for?

■ How would you sum up the atmosphere of this passage in a few words?

Our salvation is not yet completed. There is more to come. When it is completed, not only we but the whole of creation will be liberated and filled with joy. At the centre of it will be our relationship with God as members of his family.

When will this happen? The central, decisive moment will be Jesus' second coming. Then come resurrection and judgement. Then the final destruction of evil, death, sin and all that spoils God's purposes. Then new heavens and new earth.

Every book in the New Testament looks forward to this, describing it in many vivid pictures. Biblical students have disagreed on some of the details. But there is no doubt at all about the central fact.*

God told Abraham, back in Genesis 12:3, that all the nations would be blessed through him. Here it has happened. So this is our hope – new creation, the completion of God's purposes for his world and its people.

How do we respond?

Look at the following passages. What attitudes do they call for in response to the new creation?

James 5:8–9

1 Corinthians 15:58

2 Corinthians 5:9–10

---

this box continues on the next page ➡

* For a full study of this important topic see any handbook of theology, for example *Know the Truth*, Bruce Milne, IVP

"There was a great crowd, which nobody could count, from every nation and tribe and people and language, standing before the throne and before the Lamb."
Revelation 7:9

1 John 3:2–3

2 Peter 3:11,13,14,18

2 Timothy 4:1–2

Romans 8:24,25

What effect does this hope have on our understanding of mission?

The hope of the new creation gives a powerful motivation for mission. It assures us that God's purposes will be fulfilled. So our efforts are worthwhile. It gives us urgency, as we think of God's judgement (see Unit 5). It makes us want to do his will, so that we are pleasing to him. It reminds us that the whole creation is to be redeemed, so it is worthwhile for us to care for all aspects of life.

But we also need to remember that we cannot 'bring in the Kingdom' ourselves. We cannot make 'heaven on earth' or solve all the world's problems. We cannot 'build Jerusalem' here.

Only God's intervention will do that.

Between 1 and 2

We are living between the first and second comings of Jesus, between 'already' and 'not yet'.

■ Already we have experienced God's Kingdom, with its power and the signs of love and justice, freedom and salvation.
■ But it is not yet complete. We are still living in a world of sin and sorrow, sickness and imperfection.

So as Jesus said, we are sent 'into the world' to live where God has put us (John 17:18). But we are 'not of the world' (17:18) because God has redeemed us into the Kingdom of his Son (Colossians 1:13).

We have to live with this tension. But it is a creative tension.

Spend a few minutes thinking back over the whole biblical story of mission. Look at the margin diagram.

Try to express in your own words what each part tells us about mission. Use the margins if you run out of space below!

There is a further activity based on this in part B.

Creation

Fall

**Redemption
in History**

New Creation

GROUP ACTIVITY

A. Signs of the Kingdom

When Jesus came, he inaugurated the Kingdom of God. The church is the community of the Kingdom – so we can expect to see the signs of the Kingdom today. Look back at the signs of the Kingdom in the Gospels and Acts (pages 56–61). Then think of your own church or group. Which of these signs do you see today?

Which are not present?

Are there other signs of the Kingdom today, which are not mentioned?

What changes would you like to see in your church or group to make it truly the community of the Kingdom?

B. Crossing the divides

The Kingdom is for all – rich/poor, high/low, successful/failures, insiders/outsiders. The church is the community of the Kingdom. So it should be able to cross all barriers.

How does this work out in practice?

1. Which of the following do you consider important factors in enabling the church to be truly open to all?
■ the gospel is based on God's grace
■ the Kingdom of God is concerned with internal attitudes, not just external appearances
■ people enter God's Kingdom by responding to a person, rather than a principle or set of rules
■ the Kingdom is based on forgiveness and acceptance by God
■ the gospel does not require people to follow a particular culture
■ the church consists of local groups of people, with great variety in the way they work out their Christian faith in their context

2. How open is your church to 'outsiders'? Which of the following would be considered 'outsiders' by your church or group?:

■ wealthy people
■ people of another colour or race
■ modern young people with a fast lifestyle
■ middle aged people
■ people who have difficulty speaking your language
■ elderly people
■ people who are not well dressed
■ sophisticated intellectuals

What could you do to make them feel welcome into God's Kingdom?

C. Church, Kingdom, world

We have seen three views of the relationship between the church, the Kingdom and the world (page 64). Which view is closest to the view taken *in practice* by your church or group? What are the practical implications of this, in the way your church or group relates to society and the world around it?

Do you have any suggestions to give, for a better understanding, in theory and practice?

(You will have another chance to work this out in Unit 5.)

D. 'Your Kingdom come...'

What do we really mean when we pray this?

What are we expecting?

What is our role, as Christians, in helping to answer that prayer?

E. Why mission?

What is our motivation for mission? Which of the following do you consider important?

■ God's judgement and the fact that people are 'lost'
■ The hope of the Second Coming and the new creation
■ Seeking God's glory and the acknowledgement of his Kingship
■ Gratitude for what God has done for us: so we want to serve others
■ Wanting to work with God in the restoration of his creation

You may want to look at this question again in unit 5 (page 94).

GOING FURTHER

Telling the story

Look back over the whole biblical story of mission (see the margin diagram on page 66). You have already tried to express in your own words what each part of the diagram tells us about mission.

What has been new for you? What things have become clear? What questions do you have? (They may be old questions, or new ones which have been raised.)

How would you summarise the story of mission? How would you communicate it to your church or group?

- a dramatic or mime presentation?
- a song or poem?
- a parable or story?
- a case study or problem to solve?
- a game to be played?

Since the Bible tells the story dramatically, we should try to as well. Write down your ideas and outline for such a presentation, trying to relate it to your particular situation. Make a summary of about one page.

Then talk to others in your church or group (including leaders) to see how best this could be done. Perhaps it could fit into celebrations of Easter or Pentecost, or to a special event or weekend programme you are planning.

For registered students

When you have talked to others and come to some conclusions, write down your plans and send them, together with your outline, to your tutor.

The material below adds to some of the themes we looked at in Part A: the signs and extent of the Kingdom, and Paul's idea of partnership in mission.

A. The signs and extent of the Kingdom

Jesus did more than preach the Kingdom; he demonstrated its reality with 'signs of the Kingdom,' public evidence that the Kingdom he was talking about had come. We list them in

approximately the order in which they appeared, although this is not necessarily in order of importance.

Sign 1 of the Kingdom was (and still is) Jesus himself in the midst of his people (Luke 17:21; Matthew 18:20), whose presence brings joy, peace, and a sense of celebration (John 15:11; 16:33; Mark 2:18–20).

Sign 2 is the preaching of the gospel. There was no gospel of the Kingdom to proclaim until Christ arrived. Now however, that he has come, the good news of the Kingdom must be preached to all, especially to the poor (Luke 4:18, 19; 7:22).

Sign 3 of the Kingdom was exorcism. We refuse to demythologise the teaching of Jesus and his apostles about demons. Although the 'principalities and powers' may have a reference to demonic ideologies and structure, we believe that they certainly are evil, personal intelligences under the command of the Devil.

Sign 4 of the Kingdom was Jesus' healing and nature miracles – making the blind see, the deaf hear, the lame walk, the sick whole, raising the dead (Luke 7:22), stilling the storm, and multiplying loaves and fishes. We all agree that these were not only signs pointing to the reality of the Kingdom's arrival, but also anticipations of the final Kingdom from which all disease, hunger, disorder and death will be banished for ever.

Sign 5 of the Kingdom is the miracle of conversion and the new birth. Whenever people 'turn to God from idols, to serve the living and true God' (1 Thessalonians 1:9, 10), a power encounter has taken place in which the spell of idols, whether traditional or modern, and of the spirits, has been broken.

Sign 6 of the Kingdom is the people of the Kingdom, in whom is manifested that cluster of

The signs and extent of the Kingdom material is taken from the findings of the 'Consultation on the Relationship between Evangelism and Social Responsibility', held at Grand Rapids in 1982.

Christ-like qualities which Paul called 'the fruit of the Spirit.' For the gift of the Spirit is the supreme blessing of the Kingdom of God.

Sign 7 of the Kingdom is suffering. It was necessary for the King to suffer in order to enter into his glory. Indeed he suffered for us, leaving us an example that we should follow in his steps (1 Peter 2:21).

If these are the signs of the Kingdom, manifesting its present reality and pointing forward to its final consummation, how extensive is the Kingdom they signify?

In one sense, as we have seen, God's rule extends only over those who acknowledge it, who have bowed their knees to Jesus and confessed his lordship (Philippians 2:9–11). These God 'has delivered… from the dominion of darkness and transferred to the Kingdom of his beloved Son' (Colossians 1:13). Apart from them, the whole world is 'in the power of the evil one,' its 'ruler' and 'god' (1 John 5:19; John 12:31; 2 Corinthians 4:4), for 'we do not yet see everything in subjection to' Jesus (Hebrews 2:8; cf. Psalm 110:1; Acts 2:35)

Yet in another sense, the Risen Lord claimed that 'all authority in heaven and on earth' had been given to him (Matthew 28:18). For God already has 'put all things under his feet and has made him head over all things for the church' (Ephesians 1:22). His titles are 'King of kings and Lord of lords' and 'the ruler of princes on earth' (Revelations 1:5; 19:16).

How can these two perspectives be fused? How can Christ claim universal authority if the whole world still lies in Satan's power? The answer is that over his redeemed people Jesus is King *de facto*, while it is only *de jure* that he is presently King over the world, his right still being challenged by the usurper. We should reserve the expression 'the Kingdom of God' for the acknowledged rule of Christ, since this is the new thing he inaugurated at his coming, while referring to the more general 'sovereignty' of God over all things.

During the interim period between the two comings of Christ, between his victory over evil and evil's final capitulation and destruction, what should be the relations between the Kingdom community and the world?

■ First, the new community should constitute a challenge to the old. Its values and ideals, its moral standards and relationships, its sacrificial lifestyle, its love, joy, and peace – these are signs of the Kingdom, as we have seen, and present the world with a radically alternative society.

■ Secondly, as the world lives alongside the Kingdom community, some of the values of the Kingdom spill over into society as a whole, so that its industry, commerce, legislation, and institutions become to some degree imbued with Kingdom values.

The salt, light, and yeast metaphors which Jesus employed are more dynamic, since each implies the penetration of the old community by the new. The light shines into the darkness, the salt soaks into the meat, the yeast causes fermentation in the dough. So Jesus intends his followers neither to withdraw from the world in order to preserve their holiness, nor to lose their holiness by conforming to the world, but simultaneously to permeate the world and to retain their Kingdom distinctives.

Meanwhile, we do not forget that God is directly at work in his world, apart from the agency of his people. In his common grace he continues to sustain the earth and its creatures, and to give to all humankind (who bear his image and have his law written in their hearts (Romans 2:14, 15) a certain appreciation of justice, freedom, beauty, dignity, and peace.

While we gladly recognise these works of God in the world, both directly and through his people, they are not what Jesus meant by his Kingdom. It is therefore, our urgent responsibility to summon all people in Christ's name to turn and humble themselves like little children, as we have sought to humble ourselves, in order to enter the Kingdom and receive its priceless blessing, the salvation of God (Matthew 18:3).

B. Paul's idea of partnership in mission

Paul always worked with others, never alone. You can see this from Acts and from his letters. What is interesting is that Paul consciously involved people from the churches which he had founded in mission.

For example: Paul and Barnabas founded churches from which Paul then recruited members of his team, such as Timothy (Acts 16:3) and perhaps Luke (implied from Acts 16:10), Titus and others. The new church in Philippi sent support to Paul in Thessalonica (Philippians 4:15–16) and later when he was in prison. Paul's ministry in Ephesus evidently resulted in the starting of churches in the surrounding area (Acts 19:10), including perhaps Colossae and Laodicea (Colossians 1:6–8; 2:1). Paul hoped that the church in Corinth would send him on his mission to Judaea (2 Corinthians 1:16).

In Romans 15 Paul reflects on his ministry and illustrates his idea of partnership most clearly. Look at Romans 15:15–33.

■ Paul's ministry up to the present
(verses 15–22)

To whom had Paul preached up to the present? In which places? By whom was he sent? (This is not mentioned in the passage, but you know it.)

We could illustrate Paul's ministry so far like this (see margin).

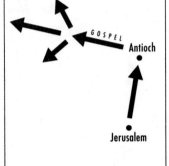

It is a fairly straightforward pattern of being sent out to found new churches, though we have already noticed how converts from these churches joined Paul.

■ Paul's new ministry (verses 23–29)

Where is Paul planning to go for his future ministry? Where is he going first, before this new mission? What kind of relationship does he want to have with the church in Rome for his ministry (see also Romans 1:13–15).

The new pattern is much more complex. Paul's purpose in going to Jerusalem was to take *money* – a collection from the Gentile churches to help the Jewish Christians in their financial difficulties (see also 1 Corinthians 16:1–4; 2 Corinthians 9:1, 12–15). The Antioch church had already done this years before (Acts 11:29)

It was a symbol for Paul of mutual

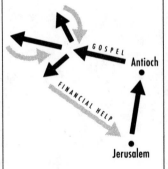

obligations and fellowship of the churches. Giving money was a response to the gospel, and acknowledgement of interdependence. Economic and spiritual blessings do not always flow in the same direction. So our diagram now looks like this (see margin).

■ Paul's request to the Romans
(verses 30–33)

Paul has already told the Romans that he would like their support for his mission to Spain. Now he asks prayer for his ministry in Jerusalem, because of the risks he faces.

He invites them to become his partners in every sense – sending him on to Spain in future, and already praying for him in Jerusalem. He also wants to minister to them (Romans 1:13–15).

It is a complex, but beautiful pattern, in which churches both received and sent the Gospel, and continued to receive and send in a relationship of mutual responsibility, according to need and opportunity (see below).

Here we see clearly that economic status and spiritual maturity have no necessary correlation. The 'mother' church receives from the 'younger' church. Those who have share with those who do not, both spiritual and economic blessings, as needed. But there is no sense of paternalism or dependence – later the roles may be reversed. It is a 'matter of equality' (2 Corinthians 8:14).

This beautiful pattern of equality and mutuality is a pattern for us to follow today. But how do we work it out in our complex world?

You can think further about this in unit 5.

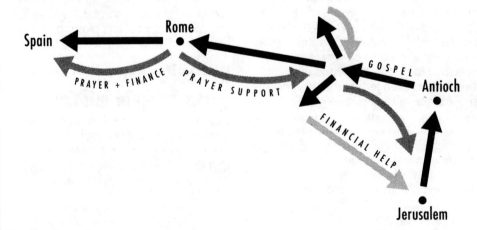

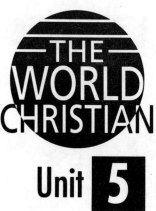

THE WORLD CHRISTIAN

Unit 5

SEVEN QUESTIONS

CONTENTS

PURPOSE

PART A The purpose of this unit is to help you to grapple with some of the key issues in the mission of the church. You will choose some of the case studies and problems in the unit and suggest answers.

PART B You will continue to work at the issues.

WHY QUESTION?

Material in this unit has been supplied by several contributors, to whom we are grateful.

Your mind is probably buzzing with questions already as you have thought about the issues facing Christians when they become involved in mission. Some of these are really puzzling – the best minds of the church down the centuries have grappled with them.

This unit contains seven key issues in mission today. (There are more that haven't been included).

Choose any one to discuss in your group, or study on your own. The seven pages that follow have questions, problems and case studies to illustrate the issues. After them you will find summary pages that bring together the key ideas, suggest possible approaches and guide you to sources for further study.

How to use the material

You will probably find it best to spend 15–20 minutes discussing the case study or problem on the first page, if you are in a group. Then look at the material at the end. This gives you a framework for approaching the issue. It may contain more questions – it will certainly include points which you will want to discuss further.

Some of the questions are closely linked, for example, 1 and 7, or 2 and 3. You will find it helpful to look at the material on the related question. If you have a larger group, you could divide into smaller groups and take up different topics.

If you are working on your own, try writing down your thoughts before looking at the summary pages.

The importance of questions

In such a short space it is impossible to do much more than raise the

questions. That is why there are suggestions for further study, which will help you to go further. So don't imagine that we have 'answered' the questions. We have just started thinking about them.

Does it matter? Does God really want us to be puzzled? Isn't it more important to be faithful in living, witnessing, sharing Christ?

But the world God has made for us is complex. And God has given us minds to think, emotions to feel, get upset or excited, wills to question and challenge. If we don't puzzle over the questions, others are certainly doing so already. And we won't be able to understand their attitudes and questions unless we have been in the same place ourselves.

The book of Job is full of questions. Job was far from 'patient' as he confronted God with what he felt was injustice. His friends, on the other hand, tried to cover up the problems by simply blaming Job. They were 'whitewashing' them. They thought that was the way to defend God's honour (Job 13:4–8). But God rebuked them for this (42:7). He also put Job in his place – not for asking questions, but for thinking that he could find all the answers, as though he were God.

So don't be afraid of asking questions! But remember that we don't have all the answers.

TAKE NOTE

You will have further chances to take up the questions in Part B of this Unit *and* in Unit 6, so you will be able to look at more than one. (You can always save up the others for another time).

REGISTERED STUDENTS

Please look at your assignment in Unit 6, part B.

IS JESUS UNIQUE?

???

➜ Also see page 80

"I am the way, the truth and the life. No one comes to the Father except through me"
Jesus, speaking in John 14:6

It seems clear, but…

"In an extraordinary way Christians have hijacked this saying and against all other evidence of Jesus' attitudes and sayings have used it as an exclusion clause to invalidate any other experience except a very narrowly conceived Christian experience."
A Methodist Minister from Birmingham

The apostles said:

"There is salvation in no other, for no other name is given in heaven or in earth whereby men may be saved"
Acts 4:12

But can that really be true? Can the large majority of humanity be wrong?

"If God really made all people and loves them, is it possible that He should leave himself without witness or confine himself to one group?"

"If the Christian gospel had moved East into India, instead of West, into the Roman empire, Jesus' religious significance would probably have been expressed by hailing him within Hindu culture as a divine avatar… "
John Hick, *God has many Names*

It seems impossible today to believe that any one person or creed can be considered absolute. Surely we have learned from all the religious wars and persecutions of the past that it is wrong to claim to have absolute truth? What I believe is true for me. What you believe is true for you. Or we could say that we each have part of the truth, not the whole.

God and elephants

Some blind men were trying to describe an elephant from what they could feel. Each of them described it differently, as…

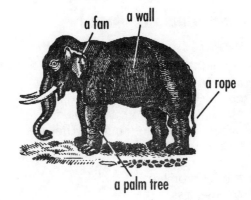

a fan a wall

a rope

a palm tree

Is this like the way in which different people describe God from their experience?

WHOSE EXPERIENCE IS TRUE?

"In the train I heard singing. In the next compartment I saw a group of young men singing hymns together. When they had finished they walked round the carriage, greeting everybody and offering them consecrated sweets.
    They told me that thy had just come from meeting their guru, called Satya Sai Baba. They told me all about him, the miracles they had seen him do, the great peace which they felt as a result of meeting him. We had a long talk together."

■ What would you say to the young men on the train?
■ Whose experience is true?
■ Is Jesus unique?
■ Is he the Truth?
■ In what sense?

Also see page 82

HOW DO WE SHOW GOD'S JUSTICE?

"God created humanity to live as persons in community. A community is a cohesive group of persons in a given area that has a sense of belonging and is bonded together by a common culture, language, interests, customs, traditions, etc."
One Gospel, Many Clothes

GROUP CONVERSION?

A Christian missionary went to live and work with a nomadic tribe in Africa. Some children from that tribe had gone to boarding schools and professed Christian faith, but none had continued on return to the tribe. He taught them everything he knew about God and the gospel. He did no social work at all.

After some time he asked those who wanted to be baptised to indicate. The whole tribe said they wanted baptism. The missionary pointed out that some had missed his sessions. The tribe replied that everyone should be baptised or no one would. The absentees had learnt from others and given their agreement.

What would you do and why?

We believe in a God of justice. But there is so much injustice in the world. How should we respond?

Do we wait for 'the world to come', when all injustices will be put right? Should we focus on preaching repentance and forgiveness, believing that that will change individuals and eventually society? Or is part of our mission to express the love and justice of God now? How should we be involved in society?

Who are we?

Our views about involvement in society are actually greatly influenced by our view of who people are.

■ Are we fundamentally *isolated individuals*, set alone on our path through life, often needing competition with others in order to overcome our natural laziness?
■ Are we *persons in community*, who find our identity as we belong to a family and community?
■ Are we *members of a corporate mass*, who have no identity apart from the collective?

Think about these alternative views as you look at these questions:

Individuals or social beings?

Should the focus of our Christian mission be on changing individuals one by one, or on addressing persons as members of a group? Think of people in your community. They may be facing issues like:
■ unemployment
■ debt problems
■ loneliness
■ pressure to succeed or to keep up with the neighbours
■ marriage and family difficulties
■ alcoholism or drugs

People experience these problems not just as individuals. The problems may be part of the experience of the group they belong to. For example if they belong to a family or group of families who are unskilled workers, they may find unemployment a more continuous problem. Whatever they face, they share in common with many others who are part of the same distinct group.

How do we show the relevance of the gospel to people in situations like these?

Working with people or for them?

Two Christian groups began to work in a slum area.

The first posted two young men to live in one of the slums and listen to the difficulties, problems and hopes of the people. The people seemed to want to have a postal address. They argued that if they had one, then the local government authority could not take their land for offices. The young men worked with them to do this. After two years they got a postal address. Then, because the people had seen success and the help of God in this area, they felt they could work together to take action to deal with other problems in the slum.

The second group discovered that the community in another slum in the same area needed a school, roads and a clinic. They brought help from the church to open a clinic and clean up the slum. The youth fellowship came and built the roads. The place soon looked cleaner and people came to the clinic. Five families came to Christ.

Which group would you commend and why?

74 UNIT 5

SHOULD WE CARE FOR THE WORLD?

3 ??? ➡ Also see page 84

■ Greenpeace volunteers jump in the water to stop whaling vessels or atomic tests. They are ready to risk their lives – some were actually killed when their ship was blown up.

■ In the foothills of the Himalayas women from the Chipko movement tie themselves to trees to prevent commercial logging. But in the same region villagers cut off branches and leaves for fuel, destroying the trees in the process. The energy crisis is far worse for them than for those who consume electricity or oil.

■ Around the world factories pour out waste and chemicals into our environment. The poor suffer most. But 'global warming' tells us all that the world is changing – and it may be too late to save it.

But do we need to 'save' the world? Isn't it going to be destroyed in any case (2 Peter 3:7)?

Green issues v. black and white preaching?

Should we become involved in issues of conservation, or concern for the environment? Isn't it more important to preach the good news of forgiveness and salvation from sin, while there is time?

On the other hand, many today *are* concerned for the environment because they believe that the world is actually, in some sense, divine. By exploiting it we have destroyed its delicate harmony and injured its living organism. So we have alienated ourselves from 'Mother Nature' or 'Gaia' and we are suffering accordingly.

We need to attune ourselves to the harmony of nature. We need to give up the idea that human beings are the most important: we are just a part of the cosmos, along with the rest of nature. God is 'green' and we will get closer to God when we are 'green' as well.

Some have argued that in fact it is Christianity which is to blame for the destruction of the environment.

"Especially in its Western form, Christianity is the most anthropocentric religion the world has seen. In absolute contrast to ancient paganism and Asia's religions, it not only established a dualism of man and nature but also insisted that it is God's will that man exploit nature for his proper ends."
Lynn White

How should Christians respond? Look at the situations described in the margin and below.

LESS WASTE

In most other parts of the world we are completely dependent on electricity and oil for our daily life. As a result, our vehicles pollute the atmosphere; our power stations contribute to the 'greenhouse effect'; our cool drinks from the fridge use CFCs which eat up the ozone layer...

We know we should do things like sharing vehicles and other equipment, or recycling as much as we can. But what are the practical difficulties? Can you devise a *workable* scheme for your church or group?

THE GANDAS

In a remote part of the world the Gandas live in a tropical rain forest. Their life is simple, 'primitive' by modern standards. They worship the trees as divine, but also cut them down as part of their 'slash and burn' agriculture.

Recently government and commercial interests have entered the area and begun large-scale tree-felling, primarily for a new paper factory, employing a large number of people. When the Gandas resisted they were removed from the area to camps, where many are now sick.

A group of Christians nearby had been trying for some time to contact the Gandas with the gospel, trying to show Christ's love through medical care, literacy and agricultural development. They found it difficult because the Gandas were so remote. Now they are much more accessible in the camps.

'Green' activists have also arrived, protesting against the destruction of the forests. They want the Gandas to be brought back and sympathise with their attitude to the trees. They also want to close the factory. They make a lot of use of the press and electronic media and have managed to get a bulky UN report published on the issues of the whole region.

Your church hears about the situation and asks you to visit, as you are in the area. What would you do? What advice would you give to:

■ the Christians?
■ the activists?
■ the Gandas?
■ the government / commercial interests?
■ your own church?

What biblical basis would you give for your advice in each case?

➡ Also see page 86

DID JESUS SPEAK ENGLISH?

The two '12 Easy Ways' boxes are by **Yemi Ladipo**. He is Vicar of Herne Hill Parish (in south-east London) and the Honorary Secretary for International Mission for BCMS Crosslinks.

12 EASY WAYS
FOR WESTERNERS TO OFFEND AFRICAN CHRISTIANS

1. Failure to greet people when you meet them
2. Enslavement to time
3. Lack of respect for older people
4. Pretence – not being your real self
5. Lack of loyalty to the community
6. Lack of discipline of young people
7. Inability to laugh at yourself or your country
8. Lack of hospitality
9. Leadership of women, especially in the home
10. Men and women showing passionate affection in public
11. Careless dressing on special occasions
12. Receiving gifts with your left hand

12 EASY WAYS
FOR AFRICANS TO OFFEND WESTERN CHRISTIANS

1. Failure to say 'please' and 'thank you'
2. Letting your family or important people jump the queue
3. Sex discrimination
4. Not keeping your surroundings clean
5. Lack of well-defined goals
6. Despising youth
7. Not treating people as individuals
8. Calling somebody fat
9. Being late for appointments
10. Men holding hands in public
11. Lack of concern for privacy
12. Apparent shyness of African women in public

God made everybody different. That makes life interesting, but it can create problems.

There are many ways you can offend others – look at the two boxes. Now think through these questions:

■ Does anything in the two lists surprise you? Why?
■ What lies behind these differences of behaviour? (Our culture can be observed by external actions like these. But behind them lie values, beliefs and ultimately the worldview of a culture – the basic assumptions people have about the nature of reality and of right and wrong.)
■ What can you learn about the world-view of African or Western Christians from the two lists?
■ How many of the attitudes or values implied are biblical? Are any of them incompatible with a biblical worldview? (whatever that is…)?
■ When the gospel enters another culture, what shape should it take? What will the church look like in that culture?

THE CHURCH IN MY CULTURE

CHURCH

THE CHURCH IN ANOTHER CULTURE

Think of the church in your culture. Which aspects of it are *essential* for a church in *any* culture?

CAN WE WORK TOGETHER?

Can we be partners in the worldwide mission of the church? Do we need to be? Think about the following questions…

■ Why should Christians even think of going to other countries when there are such strong and numerous churches in many countries of the world? Are they still welcome overseas?

■ Surely we don't need to send missionaries to the ends of the earth these days – there is so much to be done here in our own country. Should we rather be asking them to come and help us?

■ If missionaries are sent from our churches, how should they fit in with the churches in other countries? Who's in charge? Who makes the decisions?

■ Aren't there times when the continued presence of expatriate missionaries in the same place hinders the work of the church there?

■ 'There is nothing more interesting, exasperating and exciting than partnership' between Christians of different cultures. Can you think of some of the points of exasperation?

■ By definition mission involves movement; sending, going, moving out, travel, growth, development. There is something dynamic about mission. What happens when a mission becomes static or stationary?

■ But isn't there a danger that an organisation will develop new kinds of 'movement' just to keep itself in existence? Isn't there a time for closing down, recognising that we have outlived our usefulness?

What do you think are the main obstacles to partnership in mission today? Discuss the views expressed above.

OBSTACLES TO PARTNERSHIP

"The main obstacle to reciprocal partnership in mission lies in our attitude and mindset. Generally speaking, the Western church's attitude could be summarised in the familiar saying of expatriates in Africa – 'What can I do for you?' It assumes the posture of superiority and self-sufficiency…

For most of the Two-Thirds World church, the attitude can be summed up thus: 'What can I get for free?' This leads to perpetual dependence, lack of local goal-ownership and sometimes unintentional spiritual blackmail…

The image of poverty in Africa has been used from time to time, either by Africans themselves or by Westerners, to the point of suggesting that the church in Africa could do nothing significant without the help of the church from the West.

RAPHAEL MWITA

As long as these attitudes persist, there can never be true partnership between western and African churches, for a partnership of those who consider themselves unequal (for whatever reason) is a myth."

Yemi Ladipo

Also see page 90

THE PROMISED LAND?

"Because the Jewish people are the people of prophecy, they are the people of the land...

And we, knowing him who made the promise, totally support the people of and the land of Israel in their God-given, God-promised, God-ordained right to exist...

Any person or group of nations opposed to this right isn't just fighting Israel. But God and time itself."
The New York Times, 1976

God gave the land...

...to Abraham and his descendants. But Abraham had two sons – Isaac and Ishmael. Does the land belong to the children of Ishmael as well?

What about Abraham's spiritual children?

3 faiths, 1 land

The 'Holy Land' is sacred to *three* religions – Jews, Muslims and Christians.
■ All claim to be the 'Children of Abraham'
■ All three are monotheistic
■ All three share a common holy book

"The occupation must end..."

The basic conflict is that two groups of people claim the same land.

Anti-semitism

Christians created anti-Semitism. They couldn't forgive the Jews for crucifying Jesus. So they persecuted them bitterly.

They were also jealous of their financial success and suspicious of them for being a closed and separate community.

Christians fought and killed both Jews and Muslims in the Crusades, seeking to 'liberate' the holy city of Jerusalem from control by 'unbelievers'.

Carrots or oil?

> If the Middle East produced only carrots, we wouldn't care less what happened there...

Adapted from the remark of a Western diplomat in August 1990

The Middle East doesn't just produce carrots. It contains oil. So it is politically explosive and continually unstable.

Questions

What has all this got to do with mission? Everything. Talk to a Muslim; talk to a Jew... This subject will come up soon.

Where do you stand?

■ To whom does the land belong?
■ What attitude should Christians take to Israel?
■ How do we interpret scripture, especially the promises about the land?

WHAT ABOUT OTHER FAITHS?

➡ Also see page 92

"I have serious doubts that Jesus ever intended to start a powerful religion in competition with others. But that is what we have inherited."
A Methodist Minister from Birmingham

"All religions live up to their highest ideals. All have the common threads of love and compassion in them."

"Things came to a head about three years ago when I saw the film Gandhi. I was deeply moved by the heroism of the life of one of Asia's great leaders. This film was also a strong challenge to my belief in the uniqueness of Christianity. I saw here a non-Christian using principles found in the Scriptures in a more effective way than most Christians would In fact, the 'Christians' were the oppressors here and my sympathies were with the oppressed, most of whom were non-Christians."
Ajith Fernando, Sri Lanka

If we believe that Jesus is unique (see question 1), how do we relate to people of other faiths? Are they totally wrong? Do we condemn them?

Most important, what does God think about them? How will he judge?

A God of love would never condemn someone to hell

Many unbelievers are better than Christians!

It's not your creed but your <u>sincerity</u> that counts...

You <u>can't</u> blame people who don't even know the gospel!

What will happen to people at the end? Will God judge? How do we relate now to people of other faiths?

INNOCENT SUFFERING

'The more I have thought about it, the more I find myself concluding that the majority of people who suffer in the world are innocent and don't deserve it. For example, most of the multitudes that the Red Guards got rid of during the Cultural Revolution in China were not terrible criminals... The terrible suffering that tens of thousands experienced in Cambodia under Pol Pot was surely not because they had been specially wicked. They were ordinary, innocent Khmer. What did the six million Jews who died in the last war do wrong... ? Even among my own neighbours here, I can think of tons of nice people who go through horrible experiences that they really do not deserve."

"I find it too hard to believe that those who have had such a raw deal in this life will go to Hell when they die, just because they are not Christians. God is a just God. Surely this innocent suffering counts for something in his eyes..."

Quoted in *God that's Not Fair!* Dick Dowsett

This material is by **Ram Gidoomal**. He is a business consultant and became a follower of Christ from a Hindu background.

THREE POPULAR VIEWS

Here are three popular views about the world's religions:

■ **All religions are relative** they all contain *some* truth, but not absolute truth
■ **All religions are essentially the same**
■ **All religions are attempting to meet the same human needs** and some are more effective than others

Which view do you take? Or do you have another view?

IS JESUS UNIQUE?

What you believe about this question will affect your whole attitude to life and to mission. Remember the questions that we raised in Unit 2 about missionaries today (pages 28 and 29). Many believe that they are not needed, because they do not believe that Jesus is truly unique.

In this section we are looking at the question 'How do we know what is true?' In section 7 we look at the practical implications.

We can group Christian answers to this first question under three broad headings (some of the key exponents of each view are mentioned in brackets):

■ **Pluralists** believe that all religious views are equal. They each have different emphases. God is at the centre (not Christianity) and different religions reflect him in different ways, because of their different cultural backgrounds (John Hick, Stanley Samartha).
■ **Inclusivists** believe that Jesus is unique, but they believe that people who do not know him can also be saved through him. They are 'anonymous Christians', receiving Christ's salvation without yet knowing or acknowledging him (Raymondo Panikkar, Karl Rahner).
■ **Exclusivists** believe that God has revealed himself uniquely in Jesus. Salvation is only through submitting ourselves to Christ and trusting only in God's mercy and grace through him. Otherwise we are still in sin and rebellion against God (Hendrik Kraemer).

How do we evaluate these views?

We need to grapple with the issues of pluralism and relativism which are the predominant approaches to truth in the world today. For most people,

everything is relative. There is no such thing as absolute truth. It seems so intolerant.

But here are a few comments on this idea of pluralism:

1. To say that there is no absolute truth is itself an absolute statement! 'Relativist' people are usually tolerant of everything and everybody except those who question their 'relative' view of truth. Then it becomes absolute.

2. The 'majority view' is not necessarily the truth, either. If we could develop a consensus view acceptable to the majority, that would not necessarily be more true than existing minority views. Our beliefs and convictions are not objects but instruments with which we live and work. Majority opinion is certainly not the best measure of truth for us.

3. Jesus was born into a world that was just as pluralist as today. There were countless beliefs and religions. Many were relativists; they picked and chose, like the Athenians who loved to hear about 'the latest thing' (Acts 17:21). If it is not right to claim that Jesus is the only way to God, then the early Christians were mistaken. Nobody should have become a Christian.

The gospel did spread to India in the early centuries (perhaps even the 1st century AD) The early Indian Christians could easily have added Jesus to the local pantheon. But they insisted on his uniqueness.

4. It is a plain fact that different religions do not believe the same things.
■ If Muslims believe that Allah is arbitrary…
■ If Hindus believe that Brahman is

impersonal…
- If Christians believe that God is constant and personal…
- If Buddhists believe that there is no God…

are these views the same? Are they compatible with each other?

Some Christian approaches to other religions

Christian pluralist views are similar to the views above. They look for an even broader 'ecumenical movement' which will include the world religions and not just Christian denominations.

Some other Christian viewpoints:
- Other religions are delusions of the Devil. They are entirely false and we should reject them.
- Other religions contain much that is true and good.
- Other religions contain truth – for all truth is from God – but also falsehood and demonic elements.

Sir Norman Anderson comments:

"There are elements of truth which must come from God himself, whether through the memory of an original revelation, through … cross-fertilisation with some other religions, or through some measure of self-disclosure… to those who truly seek him. But there are also elements which are definitely false… Yet again, there is much that could best be described as human aspirations after the truth…"
Christianity and World Religions

What do you think?

How do we decide what is true?

For Christians our starting point is the Scriptures, which are our authority. But we must interpret them in a way that is consistent with human reason and experience.

So we must take seriously the Bible's teaching that God has revealed himself uniquely in Jesus Christ – a belief that is based on the whole Bible, Old and New Testaments. When Jesus came into the world, something unique and

unrepeatable happened. Nothing has been the same since.

So our knowledge of God and of the truth is not based on our experience or ideas (which are fallible), but on what God has revealed to us about himself, supremely in Jesus Christ. This is the decisive difference between Christian faith and all other views about God. Look at passages like Hebrews 1:1–2; 2 Corinthians 4:6; John 1:18.

This does not mean that there is no other revelation of God. 'Undeniably God works and has worked in man outside the sphere of biblical revelation', says Hendrik Kraemer, one of the main exponents of the exclusivist view.

(Kraemer, Religion and the Christian Faith, London, Lutterworth Press, p.232).

The Bible itself speaks of God's self-revelation in nature, in history, in conscience, in his image in every person.

But that revelation is of a different character from God's unique revelation in Christ. So the incarnation is the criterion by which we discern God's activity in the world and in history. We evaluate all other views in the light of Christ.

So what?

If we do believe that Jesus is unique, that He is the only Saviour, then what practical effect does this have for us? What do you think are the implications?

Here are some suggestions. Can you add to them?

We need to…

- avoid arrogance or superiority – we are not any better than others
- be open and willing to learn from others
- be sensitive and ready to listen
- demonstrate our faith practically by our love
- share our beliefs freely as we have opportunity

See question 7 for further discussion of the practical implications.

Hmm. Now where's Buddhism?

FURTHER READING

What's So Unique about Jesus? Chris Wright, Monarch Publications,1990 (An All Nations Booklet)
Christianity and World Religions – the Challenge of Pluralism, Sir Norman Anderson, IVP, 1984

HOW DO WE SHOW GOD'S JUSTICE?

This material is by **Chris Sugden**, Resident Director of the Oxford Centre for Mission Studies

There has been an international debate among evangelical Christians since the Lausanne Covenant of 1974 on the relation between proclamation of the word and the expression of Christian love and justice.

A number of important statements have been made by Christians together from all around the world. Here is one formulation of the gospel with relevance to God's love and justice. As you read it compare it with your own understanding of the gospel.

The whole gospel

"The good news is that God has established his Kingdom of righteousness and peace through the incarnation, ministry, atoning death and resurrection of his Son, Jesus Christ. The Kingdom fulfils God's purpose in creation by bringing wholeness to humanity and of creation. In the Kingdom people receive by grace alone a new status before God and people, a new dignity and worth as his daughters and sons, and empowerment by his Spirit to be stewards of creation and servants of one another in a new community. The Kingdom will come in its fulness in a new heaven and a new earth only when Jesus returns." *The Social Concern Track* at Lausanne II 1989*.

Compare this statement with your study of the Kingdom of God in Unit 4. Do you find any differences?

How would you express the Gospel and its results? Is your view as comprehensive as the Bible's?

Think about these themes, which are all part of the 'upside-down kingdom' we looked at in Unit 4:

- Individual conversion (John 4:1–38 – note how the woman is inter-related with her community)
- Religious reality (Matthew 23:23–26)
- Concern for the neighbour (those of a different community – Luke 10:25–37)
- Overcoming barriers of class, race and gender (Galatians 3:28; Ephesians 2:14–18)
- Enabling people to discover and use their talents and gifts (Matthew 25:14–30; Romans 12:3–8)
- Forgiveness and reconciliation with those whom we perceive to be enemies or who perceive us as enemies (Romans 5:8; 15:7)
- Demonstrating the reality of our faith in good works (Ephesians 2:8–10).

Are they part of your understanding of the gospel?

Living the Kingdom

How do people in the world feel the impact of the Kingdom here and now? It must be through the church, which is the principal and definitive sign and agent of the Kingdom. (This does not exclude the fact that God can use non-Christians to further his work). What the Kingdom of God means for the whole world must be seen in the church, the redeemed people of God.

The expression of the Lordship of Christ (the King of the Kingdom) over his people should be seen in the following dimensions:

1. Empowering people through the good news of the Kingdom (the gospel)
   - to experience new worth and identity as God's daughters and sons
   - to express their calling as human

* The full statement is reproduced in *Transformation – An International Dialogue on Evangelical Social Ethics*, July 1990. Supporting material is in *Transformation*, January 1990. Both available from the Paternoster Press, 3 Mount Radford Crescent, Exeter, EX2 4JW.

A COMMUNITY CELEBRATION

This story is set in a prosperous city. Some areas of government housing with low income families have become ghettoes of the underprivileged. A sense of intimidation and even violence makes the people feel isolated. Families are shut in on themselves. Young people take to the streets. There is a real absence of Christian presence and witness. These areas are generally abandoned by the churches as they are very hard to penetrate with the gospel.

A group of Christians formed a church in one of these neighbourhoods by moving in to live there. As they were all outsiders, it took many months before they could even begin conversations with the residents. They found it very difficult to find any point of prolonged contact.

The Christians demonstrated real sharing between their families. They exhibited a sense of community, in sharp contrast to the isolation existing in the housing estate. The government social services department found it a difficult place with many social problems. They tried to meet some of the needs by appointing a recreation officer and building a recreation hall. Even after a year, he was unable to bring about any community participation in recreation events. He was very frustrated.

The church then took responsibility for organising a community event. The thirty families in the church went out and invited the others to an evening of fun and celebration on their national holiday.

Out of curiosity about these people who seemed to be close to each other, many families from the estate attended the celebration. They sang and danced late into the night. They forged bonds of friendship which became the basis of the church's acceptance into the community and of their witness and service.

---

beings to be the stewards of creation
2. Being reconciled to enemies
3. Working for justice with all exploited people

Here are some questions to help think this through:

Empowering and enabling others

How does your church enable people to live full lives, to be truly human? One way to find out is to ask in what ways your church is helping those who at present seem to be powerless, without influence or significance in their work, church, neighbourhood or society.

Do you feel yourself to be like that sometimes? Can you think of others who are in such a situation?

What causes such powerlessness?

God's grace brings people new identity and worth as his daughters and sons. He calls and enables them to be stewards of his creation. How should his people express this grace in practical terms?Can you think of ways in your situation?

One new movement in Christian mission is the movement for developing small income-generating projects among poor communities, often through providing credit at favourable rates to small business people, helping them to get started.

Being reconciled to enemies

Paul emphasised that Christ's victory over evil was shown as barriers between races, classes and genders were overcome (Galatians 3.28; Ephesians 2.14–18; Romans 15.7)

How are your church, family, community overcoming these barriers?

Do you know, visit, welcome people from different backgrounds?

What role do women and children have in your church life? What about men?

What relations does your church have with a social group different from most of the church members? What do you think you can learn from Christians in such a group?

Working with others for justice

One way to work for justice is to begin by building a sense of community. Look at the story in the box and see if it gives you any ideas.

What community events can you identify in the community you want to reach?

FURTHER READING

A Theology of the Kingdom in Transformation, Graham Cray

Proclaiming Christ in Christ's Way, Vinay Samuel and Albrecht Hauser, Regnum Books, Box 70, Oxford

Kingdom and Creation in Social Ethics, Oliver Barclay and Chris Sugden, Grove Ethics Series, Grove Books

Taking Action, Roy McLoughry, IVP, 1989

3 ??? SHOULD WE CARE FOR THE WORLD?

This question is closely linked with the questions about justice in question 2. The answers are based on the same belief about the nature of God's Kingdom and the kind of transformation which his Kingdom brings. So what follows is equally relevant to the issue of justice.

Belonging to who?

The simplest approach is to ask *who the world belongs to*. You can answer that from your study of the biblical story in Unit 2.

■ What does creation tell us about the world in relation to God and also to human beings?
■ What is God's position? What is ours?
■ What do the fall and redemption add to our understanding?
■ What about new creation?

As we go through the stages in the biblical story it helps us to build up an appropriate answer to the question.

Compare your thoughts with these extracts from *Transformation – The Church in Response to Human Need* – a report of Evangelical Christian agencies and churches from around the world on involvement in relief and development with poor communities (see margin).

Read them carefully, noting all the references to 'the world' or 'the earth'. They give us an idea of God's purpose for the world and our responsibility.

Owners or Stewards?

"'The earth is the Lord's and all that is in it' (Psalm 24:1). 'This land is mine' (Leviticus 25:23). All human beings are God's creatures. As made

in his image they are his representatives, given the responsibility for caring wisely for his creation. We have to confess, however, that God's people have been slow to recognise the full implications of their responsibility. As his stewards, we do not own the earth but we manage and enhance it in anticipation of Christ's return. Too often, however, we have assumed a right to use his natural resources indiscriminately. We have frequently been indifferent, or even hostile, to those committed to the conservation of non-renewable sources of energy and minerals, of animal life in danger of extinction and of the precarious ecological balance of many natural habitats. The earth is God's gift to all generations. An African proverb says that parents have borrowed the present from their children. Both our present life and our children's future depends upon our wise and peaceful treatment of the whole earth.

"When either individuals or states claim an absolute right of ownership, that is rebellion against God. The meaning of stewardship is that the poor have equal rights to God's resources (Deuteronomy 15:8–9). The meaning of transformation is that, as stewards of God's bountiful gifts, we do justice, striving together through prayer, example, representation and protest to have resources redistributed and the consequences of greed limited (Acts 4:32–5:11)."

So it is not that the earth is divine, in any sense. It does not have life or power of its own, any more than we have. But it is made by God and so it has value and we are concerned for it as God's stewards.

Does this put human beings too much at the centre? It is true that

This is available either as Grove Booklet on Ethics No 62, or with supporting papers in *The Church in Response to Human Need*, edited by Vinay Samuel and Chris Sugden (Eerdmans/Paternoster 1987).

too often we *have* put selfish and greedy human interests above the interests of the creation as a whole. But this does not mean that we can deny our special role and responsibility to care for God's creation, not dominating or exploiting but exercising responsible stewardship.

Not only development but transformation

"There are a number of themes in the Bible which help us focus on the way we understand transformation. The doctrine of creation speaks of the worth of every man, woman and child, of the responsibility of human beings to look after the resources of nature (Genesis 1:26–30) and to share them equitably with their neighbours. The doctrine of the fall highlights the innate tendency of human beings to serve their own interests, with the consequences of greed, insecurity, violence and the lust for power. 'God's judgement rightly falls upon those who do such things'. (Romans 2:2). The doctrine of redemption proclaims God's forgiveness of sins and the freedom Christ gives for a way of life dedicated to serving others by telling them about the Good News of salvation, bringing reconciliation between enemies and losing one's life to see justice established for all exploited people.

"We have come to see that the goal of transformation is best described by the biblical vision of the Kingdom of God. This new way of being human in submission the the Lord of all has many facets. In particular, it means striving to bring peace among individuals, races and nations by overcoming prejudices, fears and preconceived ideas about others. It means sharing basic resources like food, water, the means of healing and knowledge. It also means working for a greater participation of people in the decisions which affect their lives, making possible an equal receiving from others and giving of themselves. Finally, it means growing up into Christ in all things as a body of people dependent upon the work of the Holy Spirit and upon each

other."

What changes has the transforming power of God made…

■ in your own life?
■ in the lives of others you know?
■ in the atmosphere and actions of a community you are aware of?

What guidelines does this give you for working to see that transforming power extended in new ways?

A final thought

There is no dichotomy between our mission of serving Christ and proclaiming him, and our responsibility to carry out the mandate of the Creator. They are inseparable. There is no restriction of Christianity to 'church affairs'. For 'all of life comes under the rule of God and those in the Kingdom have been re-created by God *in the order of the creator.'*

What redemption does is to add a whole new dimension to that task, recognising both the devastating effects of sin and also the amazing new power of the cross, resurrection, forgiveness of sins and presence of the Holy Spirit. So both the *announcement of God's rule* with his glorious new offer to men, and the *working out of his rule* in every area of life are inescapable parts of our Christian duty. The dichotomy between sacred and secular, spiritual and material, has gone. All the world is ours, to reclaim for our King, who will return to consummate his kingdom.

Questions and tensions still remain, but these are not between the spiritual and material but between the 'already' and the 'not yet', Christ's present victory over sin and the continuing presence of sin. We are living in the 'overlap' between the ages.

We looked at Romans 8:18–25 in Unit 4 (page 65). There is no better passage to sum up the tension between our present responsibility for our groaning world and our hope for its glorious liberation through Christ.

FURTHER READING

Meeting God in Creation, Lawrence Osborn, Grove Spirituality Series No 32, Grove Books, 1990.

Green Finger of God, Maurice Sinclair, Paternoster.

Issues Facing Christians Today, John Stott, Marshall Pickering, revised edition, 1990.

DID JESUS SPEAK ENGLISH?

"Contextualisation takes place when the presentation and outworking of the gospel is done in such a way as to be appropriate to the context in which it is found. That context may be Athens or New York or a remote village in Sri Lanka. Contextualisation becomes necessary whenever we work with a person of a culture different from ours."
Ajith Fernando, *Jesus and the World Religions*, STL/ MARC

Culture has been defined as: 'an integrated system of *beliefs* (about God or reality or ultimate meaning), of *values* (about what is true, good, beautiful and normative), of *customs* (how to behave, relate to others, talk, pray, dress, work, play, trade, farm, eat, etc.), and of *institutions* which express these beliefs, values and customs (government, law courts, temples or churches, family, schools, hospitals, factories, shops, unions clubs, etc.), which binds a society together and gives it a sense of identity, dignity, security, and continuity'
(*The Willowbank Report – Gospel and Culture*, Lausanne Occasional Paper 2, LCWE).

The gospel: with or without chopsticks?

External behaviour and customs in any culture reflect its inner world view.

How do we translate the gospel into that world view?

Once people from that culture have accepted the gospel, how do they express their new faith in a way that is compatible both with the gospel and their traditional world view? How much of their world view, beliefs, values have to change? And how do they express those changes? Do they adopt the behaviour of the people from whom they received the gospel?

Do people need to put on ties, eat with chopsticks, say 'please' and 'thank you', line up in queues, eat meat, get up early or kiss their wives in public? Are any of these part of the gospel?

Making the gospel fit

Adapting the gospel to fit another culture is often called 'contextualisation'.

This could happen anywhere: middle class people trying to witness to inner city neighbourhoods; educated people witnessing to people in backward rural situations; village evangelists relating to sophisticated young people.

The danger of syncretism

The great danger in such efforts is always syncretism. Ajith Fernando:

UNITY OR DIVERSITY?

An evangelist works among middle class caste Hindu farmers in a group of villages in South India. The farmers live in houses in the main part of the village. On the edge, usually across the stream, is a collection of small huts where the outcaste people live, called the *cheri* or slum. They do things like collecting rubbish or skinning animals for leather, which are considered menial and unclean. If there are any Christians in the village, they live there, because they are from that background.

The farmers would never dream of becoming Christian or joining the church. It would mean leaving their community and joining that one – a disgraceful thing to do.

The evangelist visits the farmers and their families in their homes. He does not usually visit the Christian homes in the *cheri*. He talks to them about Jesus. When they respond he doesn't talk about the church but tells them to pray to Jesus in their home, with their family and neighbours. Later he takes them to meet people from the same background in other villages. When they are ready, he baptises them in another centre, away from their village.

Over the years, several hundred have been baptised. Now some new churches have been built in the main parts of the villages.

Are these people being exclusive? What about mixing with people of other castes? Will they be willing to eat with them, or to get married to them? Do you agree with this approach? What cultural values is it trying to safeguard? What are its dangers?

'Contextualisation must be distinguished from syncretism. Syncretism takes place when, in the presentation and outworking of Christianity, elements essential to the gospel are dropped or elements incompatible with the gospel are taken on in the efforts to identify with non-Christians. Syncretism took place when the pagan idea of white supremacy was adopted by the church so that it supported segregation. It takes place when a Christian, trying to maintain his friendship with a non-Christian participating in a peace march, worships with the rest when they pass a Hindu shrine. It takes place each time a Christian turns to an astrological guide for direction in his or her life. It takes place when Christians condone indiscriminate abortion and euthanasia because of a secular humanistic approach to the sanctity of human life.'

There are essential aspects of the gospel that are relevant to all cultures and cannot be changed. We need to identify these as we communicate.

How many cultures?

People sometimes think that in order to communicate effectively with another culture, you just need to know your Bible and that culture. Some missionaries have assumed that their task is simply to bring 'the gospel' to 'another culture'.

They do not realise that their experience of the gospel is the gospel *in their culture*. Unconsciously they pass on *that* form of the gospel to the other culture. This especially happens when we assume that our culture is 'Christian' or better than another.

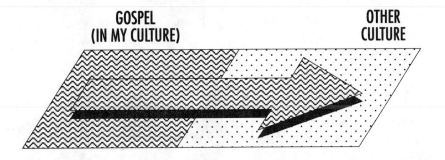

We need first to understand our own culture in order to see how it has affected our understanding of the gospel (and how the gospel has affected our culture). Then we can look for ways to relate the gospel to the other culture as well. So two cultures are involved, *both* in relation to the Bible and the gospel.

Some would say three cultures, because the Bible itself comes out of another culture.

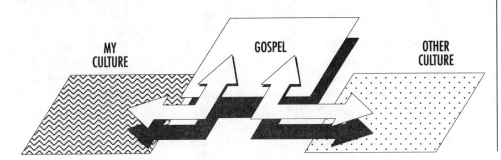

The church comes in many shapes
What shape does the church have in another culture? Look at the case study in the box.

FURTHER READING

Down to Earth, John Stott and Robert Coote, (eds), Hodder & Stoughton, 1981 (contains the Willowbank Report).

Mission and Culture, Bill Cotton, chapter 5 of *Into All the World*, Harold Rowdon (ed), Paternoster, 1989.

One Gospel, Many Clothes, Chris Wright and Chris Sugden (eds), EFAC/Regnum, 1990 (available from Paternoster).

5
? ? ?

CAN WE WORK TOGETHER?

This material is by **Stanley Davies**, General Secretary of the Evangelical Missionary Alliance in the UK.

PARTNERSHIPS THAT WORK

Jonelle is a French-English missionary, skilled in the Khmer language. In Cambodia before the Khmer Rouge came to power there was a well-known composer of youth songs named Mao Vinna. Before he died he had trained a young man named Mr Pran, who could not only write music but also had mastered complicated Khmer poetry.

Jonelle introduced Mr Pran to a computer programme that could handle Khmer script, and Australian Christians provided him with a computer. So he was able to produce a hymnbook of 283 hymns that will nourish Khmer congregations around the world.

In Nepal, Afghanistan, and several other countries, united missions have become the norm. Groups working in that country have pooled their resources and relate together, to the government, to the church (where it exists) and other agencies in the country.

Can you think of other examples of partnership, at different levels or different stages?

World mission is the privilege and responsibility of the church in every place. And as the church exists, in one form or another, around the world, we cannot think any more of of working on our own. We have to work in partnership.

There are at least three different levels of partnership in world mission:

Level 1
World mission is a partnership between the triune God – Father, Son and Holy Spirit – with his church on earth. What an incredible privilege to be 'workers together with God'.

Level 2
World mission is a partnership between those who are sent out beyond the church's immediate area and those who remain at the local level. This is a partnership between the sent and the senders.

Level 3
World mission is a partnership between those who are sent from their own church in our country to those in other countries. This happens first in primary evangelism, where there are no churches, and later with the churches in that country.

Paul's partnership
Paul, in his letter to the Philippians, speaks of partnership in several ways:

■ **Partnership in God's grace**
Philippians 1:7 – 'You are all joint partners in my ministry of grace' (paraphrase by FF Bruce). This is serving grace rather than saving grace.
■ **Partnership in the Gospel**

Philippians 1:5 – Paul enjoyed team work with other believers.
■ **Partnership in prayer** Philippians 1:4 & 1:19 (also see Romans 15:30–32; 2 Corinthians 1:10–11 and Ephesians 6:19–20).
■ **Partnership in suffering** Philippians 1:7 & 4:4 (see also Philippians 3:10 & 1:29).
■ **Partnership in giving** Philippians 4:16–18 (see also 2 Corinthians 8:1–6). Partnership requires us to receive as well as to give.

Stages in developing partnership
Harold Fuller describes four stages in developing partnership.

PIONEER   PARENT

PARTNER   PARTICIPANT

Another model is to recognise that there is the need to take a series of steps from dependence through to interdependence. See the diagram at the top of the next page.

While both these models can be helpful, there is a danger that we assume that there has to be a stage of dependence, or that we have to act as 'parents' in early stages, rather than just pioneers. Yemi Ladipo comments:
"If one partner sees himself as a

DEPENDENCE		INDEPENDENCE		INTERDEPENDENCE
We want you because we need you to do what we can't do		We don't want you because we don't need you because we can do what we have to do		We want to welcome you so that we can discover that we need each other

FURTHER READING

Ripening Harvest: Gathering Storm, Maurice Sinclair, chapter 6 – 'Partnership in Mission'.

Mission – Church Dynamics, Harold Fuller, William Carey Library

One Passionate Purpose, OMF Books, pp.16–22

The Cost of Reciprocal Partnership in World Mission, Yemi Ladipo, BCMS Crosslinks.

See also Unit 8

parent, there cannot be a partnership between equals. It is this kind of approach which has created problems… It can be said to be the source of all paternalism and perpetual dependency. Mission is the work of the Holy Spirit and a true partnership should begin from the moment the gospel was first preached, following St Paul's model; entrusting local leadership to the local Christians and then leaving… **To my mind, a healthier, and more accurate, model for partnership would consist of three stages: Pioneer, Participant, Partner**."

 What do you think?

Working at partnership

Look back to the material in Unit 4 about Paul's pattern of mission (pages 69 and 70). Paul not only gave them leadership but involved them with him in mission.

It is easy to blame the colonial past, or present economic disparities, for tensions in partnership. The truth is that we always need to *work* at partnership, because it is a reciprocal relationship, which requires mutual respect.

As Maurice Sinclair says:

"For the global partnership to work it must be a partnership of reconciliation, understanding, mutuality, prayer and suffering. Only then will it fully and truly be a partnership of reaping."

Whether it is Africans with Chinese, Australians with Scots, Brazilians with Arabs, Americans with Japanese, or Tamils with Gujerathis, we all have to work at partnership.

Increasingly, there is a growing commitment by Great Commission Christians to work together to make Christ known to all peoples everywhere.

"Authentic partnership is actually between two crippled partners – the blind and the lame – who cannot go on a journey unless the lame person provides eyes for the blind and the blind person provides legs for the lame. Most partnership is not worked out by sitting and talking about it. It is worked out by setting out on the journey."
Vinay Samuel and Chris Sugden

"Lasting partnerships only occur when we identify a common objective that is larger than the resources of any of our individual ministries."
Interdev

"'Mission out of poverty' can have advantages over 'Mission out of affluence.'"
Theodore Williams

WHAT AFRICA CAN OFFER IN PARTNERSHIP

The African church may have little 'gold' to offer (because the bulk of her supply is in the wrong hands in South Africa!). In any case, we have a saying in Africa, that 'If all a thing costs you is money, that thing must be cheap indeed.'

We have plenty of 'frankincense' – what with six million additional church members annually, we have lots of the aroma of Christ to share with the world in depth of human relationship. We may not build high but we do dig deep. We are experienced in spiritual midwifery!

Finally, the African church can offer the world plenty of 'myrrh'. We can share how to make do with little, and how to endure suffering and deprivation without losing sight of God who in Christ 'holds everything together' (Colossians 1.17). There is room for suffering in African theology and a strong affirmation that nothing can separate us from the love of God.

Yemi Ladipo, *The Cost of Reciprocal Partnership in World Mission* (An African perspective).

THE PROMISED LAND?

WHO LIVED IN PALESTINE WHEN?

- **2000-539 BC** Abraham to the exile (most of the O.T.)
- **539 BC-135 AD** Under Persian, Greek and Roman domination. (The temple was finally destroyed in AD 70. After a further revolt, Jerusalem was again destroyed in AD 135.)
- **135-1918 AD** Under the rule of Romans, Byzantines, Arabs and Turks (including the time of the Crusades)
- **1881 to the present** The period of the return of the Jewish people to the land (beginning from 1881)

GOD'S PROMISE TO ABRAHAM

What does the Bible say about the promise of the land (first to Abraham in Genesis 12.3)?

- Was it unconditional? Did the people of Israel have any obligations to fulfil?
- Were the promises to Israel fulfilled in Christ, the true representative of Israel?
- Were the promises to Israel fulfilled in the church (described as Israel in the New Testament)?

Approaching the subject

No other issue raises so many questions in one:

- human rights and justice
- minority rights
- prejudice (racial, religious, political…)
- imperialism (Western? Christian?)
- interpreting the Bible
- the land
- prophecy
- Israel and the church
- fulfilment in Christ
- evangelism and witness
- living with the past

This topic is sure to provoke heated discussion, and usually more heat than light.

Whose land?

Where do we begin in approaching it? One of the most helpful studies published is W*hose Promised Land?* by Colin Chapman, published by Lion.

We have followed its approach. Please read this book or any comparable study, because we cannot do more here than list the questions. To try and give answers in this short space would be to over-simplify, which is one of the major reasons for continuing disagreement.

The history

We need to look first at the the historical facts: who has lived in the land and when? Look at the material in the margin.

It is important to be clear about these historical details – though they do not necessarily lead to clear answers. Both Jews and Palestinians have lived in the land over many periods. It depends how far back we take our starting point to assess the respective claims.

Listening to the viewpoints

What have been the perspectives and roles of the different groups? For example, Jewish settlers, Zionists, Palestinians, non-Zionist Jews, other Arabs, the Eruropean powers after the First and Second World Wars…?

These, too, are very varied. Each has valid insights and arguments, based on their perspective and experience. We have to listen to all and weigh what they say.

How do we interpret biblical prophecy?

- Do we take it all as *literal prediction*? That is the position of some, but it is very difficult to maintain consistently for all prophecy. It would include the rebuilding of the Temple and the restoration of animal sacrifices, as well as all that is described in the book of Revelation (a book of prophecy, see Revelation 1:3; 22:18)
- Do we take it all as *symbolic prediction*? In that case we do not need to look for literal fulfilment. But some predictions *have* been fulfilled literally: for example, the birth of Jesus the Messiah; the scattering of the people of the northern and southern kingdoms of Israel and Judah; the destruction of Babylon and so on.
- How do we decide *when* a prediction has been fulfilled, partially or completely? For example, when a small number of people returned to Jerusalem at the time of Cyrus, was this the fulfilment of the prophecies of a glorious return?
- Do we assume that biblical prophecy is all about prediction and foretelling the future? Should we be looking for the *principles* behind what the prophets declared? They referred to specific events and

situations and that gave their words a biting contemporary relevance. That showed that God was sovereign and active, able to intervene. They also told the people what God required from them – their repentance or obedience or some other ethical or spiritual response. That was the purpose for their message.

■ What about the *fulfilment of prophecy in Christ*? Jesus himself said, 'Today this scripture has been fulfilled in your hearing…' (Luke 4:21). He told his disciples that all that the prophets said was being fulfilled in and through him – including what they said about Israel and its redemption. (Luke 24:21,27, 44–47). This does not mean that there is nothing more to happen for the fulfilment of God's purposes. The apostles referred to events that were still to take place (Acts 3:21). But it does mean that everything in the Old Testament (and New Testament) prophecies must be understood in the new light of Christ and his coming.

So as we look at biblical prophecy and try to understand the place of Israel and the land, we have to do so in the light of Christ and the re-interpretation that he brought. This raises the whole question of the relationship between Israel and the church.

Israel and God

In what sense is the nation of Israel today the fulfilment of God's purpose? If we believe that God still has a special purpose for the people of Israel, because of his promises (Romans 11:1,28), does that mean that we are to support uncritically all that the modern nation of Israel does today? What is God's ultimate purpose for the people of Israel?

Some biblical principles

These are hard questions and there are no easy answers…!

If we take the 'easy' way out by simply identifying ourselves with one side or another, we will find ourselves caught in a position where we cannot communicate with the other side – and may not really be helping those we think we are

supporting.

Because there are some other key biblical principles for us to apply:

■ **Justice** The prophets are full of it. Both sides in this conflict are looking for it and deserve it.
■ **The needs of minorities** The Old Testament is on the side of the weak, such as the poor, widows and orphans. It specifically includes resident aliens and other minorities in this category (eg. Leviticus 19:10,33,34). The prophets took up the theme and so did the apostles (Acts 6:1;James 1:27) Both Jews and Palestinians have been in this position. Both have suffered.
■ **The relationship between people** of different religions, races, cultures, languages in the same country. Can a nation be based on one religion,race or culture? How do you reconcile the interests of different groups in the same nation?

This is not a problem just for Israel/Palestine. We find it all around the world.Any state based exclusively on religion or culture faces intolerable problems.
■ **Suffering, repentance, forgiveness** These are fundamental biblical themes. What place do they have in facing the issues of the Middle East (and any other conflict situation)? Perhaps they are the missing key to the whole issue.

Elias Chacour is a Palestinian Christian. In his book *Blood Brothers* he describes his perspective, as one who has suffered deeply. But he also speaks of his attempts at reconciliation and justice, based on suffering, love and forgiveness.

There is plenty of room for repentance, for all involved – Christians, Jews, Muslims. Nobody comes out with a clear record.

The peacemakers are God's children. But they frequently face suffering for their efforts.

CHRISTIAN QUESTIONS

Questions for Christians raised by the problems of the Middle East:

1. How do we account for the break between the Church and the Synagogue in the 1st and 2nd centuries?
How do we understand the process of mutal rejection which took place?
2. How do we understand – biblically and theologically – the relationship between the Jewish people and church?
3. How do we understand anti-semitism? In the light of all that Christians have contributed to anti-semitism in the past, how do we cope with our collective guilt as Christians? How do we respond to contemporary manifestations of anti-semitism?
4. What sympathy do we have for the aspirations of the Jews through many centuries of their dispersion for a land, and their more recent aspirations for nationhood?
5. Is it possible to distinguish between the basic vision of Zionism and the way in which Jews and Israel have actually tried to make their dream a reality?
6. What is our hermeneutical key for working out a Christian interpretation of Old Testament prophecies and promises?
7. What does it mean to share the gospel with the Jew today – both in Israel and in the dispersion?
8. What is our eschatological vision for the future of the Jewish people and for the church?
9. How do we as Christians respond to issues of human rights and injustice?
10. Does Christianity have any solution to the problem of minorities? What kind of record does the church have in its dealings with minorities?

Colin Chapman

FURTHER READING

Whose Promised Land? by Colin Chapman, Lion, 1983, revised

WHAT ABOUT OTHER FAITHS?

Ajith Fernando works with Christians, Buddhists, Hindus and others in Sri Lanka. He has made a careful study of Paul's attitude to other religions, based on his encounter with the Athenians in Acts 17:16–34. (We looked very briefly at this in unit 4, page 62.)

A spirit provoked

He describes Paul's first response as 'a spirit provoked'. Paul was 'greatly distressed' at the idolatry which he saw (Acts 17:16). In this he was following the Old Testament condemnation of idolatry. It takes away from the glory of God, the Creator.

Paul makes this very clear in Romans 1:18–32, where he shows the disastrous results of idolatry.

So Paul's response was to 'reason' and 'discuss' with people. He did not keep his views to himself. From the rest of Acts and his letters, we see his eagerness to proclaim the good news of Jesus. Romans 1:14–16 is his motto: 'I am under obligation… I am eager to preach… I am not ashamed of the gospel… '

So sharing the good news about Jesus is our primary responsibility to people of every background. The glory of God is our supreme motivation.

A spirit restrained

But the rest of this passage shows 'a spirit restrained'.

Paul did not condemn or criticise the Athenians – instead he complimented them on their religious feeling and sincerity (17:22). He then reasoned with them, sharing with them from their own reason the truth about the One Creator God. Then he moved on to speak from the evidence of history – God's unique revelation in Jesus.

This is how Ajith Fernando sums up Paul's attitude.

"On the one hand there is a firm belief in the wrongness of life apart from Christ. On the other hand there is a respect for all individuals because they are intelligent human beings endowed by God with the privilege and responsibility of choosing to accept or reject the gospel. This caused Paul to reason with them about the truth of God. This combination of a strong conviction about truth and a respect for the individual … forms one of the foundational principles in formulating our attitude to other faiths."

(Ajith Fernando, *Jesus and the World Religions*)

Dialogue

This approach led Paul to dialogue with people of other faiths. The same Greek word is used in Acts 17:17. It means to 'discuss' or 'reason' with another person.

Much has been written about 'dialogue' with people of other faiths. Some believe this is the *only* way to relate to each other – to come together in openness to each

> **"If we have grasped (or been grasped by) something that is true, the experience is not something which we should keep to ourselves. For the first Christians it was not something they could keep to themselves. To treat the story of Jesus as if it were merely private and personal would have robbed it of its public, universal importance."**
>
> *Relations with People of Other Faiths*, published by the British Council of Churches, 1983

other, ready to listen, to learn, to be convinced. For some people, true dialogue is not possible unless I am willing to come without presuppositions, without assuming that I am right, ready to give up my beliefs if the other convinces me.

Others reject dialogue as compromise. What is needed is proclamation, they say.

Ajith Fernando (and others) show the place of genuine discussion (dialogue) in order to have real communication.

In this dialogue, we come to the other person to listen, to understand. We accept that it is possible to learn from the other. We are ready to admit our mistakes, to learn that others have not understood us, or disagree with us. We genuinely want to know what the other person believes or feels. We are also ready to ask questions which will help us to know whether the other person has understood what we believe and feel.

This kind of dialogue is based on the fact that we are all human beings, made in the image of God. It creates respect and trust. It removes misunderstandings. It enables people truly to hear and encounter each other. It does not involve any compromise of belief, on either side. And it is hard and sometimes painful to practise.

A group of Muslims and Christians met for three days to 'dialogue' about their responses to Salman Rushdie's book. Their time together was televised. It was moving to see them change from accusation and confrontation to trust, as they shared their deepest feelings, their hurt and pain and misunderstandings. At the end they did not agree on what should be done. But they understood and trusted each other.

FURTHER READING

Jesus and the World Religions, Ajith Fernando, STL Books/MARC, 1988 (highly recommended)
What About Other Faiths? Martin Goldsmith, Hodder and Stoughton, 1989
Christianity and Other Faiths, Paternoster, 1983

HOW WILL GOD JUDGE?

For generations it was virtually assumed that God would call everyone to account for their lives, and many were profoundly concerned that they could end up in Hell. Not so today. We now question whether God has the right to examine us, and assume that fairness demands universal acquittal.

Part of the problem is that very few people from a nominally Protestant cultural background have ever been afraid of God. We do not understand the Israelite's terror in the presence of God's demanding holiness (Exodus 20:18). We sing of God's purity with none of Isaiah's awful sense of lostness (Isaiah 6:4f). We long for the glory of the Lord, but we are bewildered that the shepherds found it so terrifying (Luke 2:8f) Hardly any of us have trembled before God. Is it surprising that we misrepresent him?

It is not that we need to replace our concept of God's grace and love with that of his holiness and wrath. Rather we need to repent of our dilution of both. For if we trivialise God's attitude to sin we will never grasp the sheer wonder of his grace.

God's judgement

Read Romans 2:1–5, 12–16, and notice the fairness of the standards of God's judgement.

1. He judges people by their standards of criticising others.
2. He judges by what people know from the way they are made.
3. He judges by the standards of the individual's conscience.
4. He judges people as they really are.

In other words, God lowers his standard to what people actually know – and still no one passes the exam. See Romans 3:9–20. No wonder Paul felt a profound sense of obligation to evangelise people (Romans 1:14).

Do we have too optimistic a view of human nature, as though people are really on God's side anyway, failing to respond only because of our faulty presentation techniques? The gospel states that people naturally reject Jesus, prefer darkness, and are habitually evil. It takes a miracle from above to put someone right with God. See John 3:3, 19–20, 36.

The material in this section is by **Dick Dowsett**, Bible teacher and Conference Minister with the Overseas Missionary Fellowship. He has worked for a number of years in the Philippines.

LOOK BACK...

...to your discussion of our motives for mission in unit 4, page 67. Do you want to add anything to your thoughts now?

FURTHER READING

Essentials (Chapter 6), David L. Edwards and John Stott, Hodder and Stoughton, 1988

Christianity and World Religions (Chapter 5), Sir Norman Anderson, IVP, 1984

God That's Not Fair (Chapter 5), Dick Dowsett, OMF/STL, 1984

PART B

Universalism

Can it be that the situation is not in fact as bad as this?

Many have wanted to argue that at judgement it will become clear that many who are not Christians will nonetheless be saved.

For example, in 1979 Pope John Paul II wrote:

"Man – every man without any exception whatever – has been redeemed by Christ, and ... with man – with each man without exception whatever – Christ is in a way united, even when man is unaware of it."

Undoubtedly Christ died for the sins of the world. But in the New Testament this fact was the ground of their appeal to people to be reconciled to God, lest the grace of God be wasted (2 Corinthians 5:20–6.1). Unconditional universalism may seem to fit the demands of Western logic, but apostolic teaching and practice pronounces it as tragic wishful thinking.

Will some be saved without knowing?

Other Christians have speculated about judgement. Some suggest that God judges on the basis of what he knows of how people would have responded if they had been given the chance.

Others have written of those who perhaps cast themselves on God's mercy and experience his forgiveness without at the time realising that it is based upon what was achieved by Christ's death on the cross. Such speculation is very appealing. And that is what makes it dangerous. Since the Bible does not clearly teach this, we have no way of confirming it.

We must leave the final outcome of all these questions with God. The fact is that we do not know all the answers. The Bible does not encourage us to speculate. Our responsibility is to show God's love through our friendship and humble service and to share the good news of Jesus. Our highest concern should be the glory of God.

GOING FURTHER

Choose another issue and work at it. You will find it helpful to identify:

■ The main issue
■ Other issues which are part of the main issue, or connected issues
■ Different answers that could be given to them
■ Your own answers, with reasons

Jot down your thoughts and also note any other questions that have arisen in your mind.

For Registered Students

Look at your assignment in Unit 6, Part B.

THE
WORLD
CHRISTIAN

Unit **6**

SIMULATION GAMES

CONTENTS

PURPOSE

PART A The purpose of this unit is to help you to understand how you can use simulation games to learn about mission. You will look at different kinds of games that are available and discover ways to use them.

PART B You will look at another issue from unit 5

WHAT IF...?

The deep end

The best way to learn to do anything is to try to do it. You may make mistakes, but that's the only way to learn.

It's certainly true that you can only learn to swim, ride a bicycle, drive a car or fly a plane by actually *doing* it, not just books or theory. So is the best way to learn about mission to go and do something – even if we make mistakes?

That's right. But mistakes can be expensive, for us or for others. If you throw a person 'in at the deep end' or put them behind a steering wheel on the first day, there's a risk that they might drown, or crash the car. If people rush around evangelising insensitively, others can be hurt.

There is no substitute for practical experience. But we need to prepare for the experience as much as we can beforehand.

Simulation games

An effective way to do this is through *simulating* the experience. Pilots and astronauts spend a lot of their training in simulators, where they get the feeling of flying and

learn to respond, without actually leaving the ground. It's safer, and less expensive, than actual flying.

Simulation games are used in the same way to give practice for all kinds of real life situations. They are a very good way to learn, the next best thing to the real experience.

We can use them for training and learning about mission as well. Rightly used, they can greatly enhance more traditional ways – such as listening to speakers – or even watching a video!

We have already used case studies in this book, especially in unit 5. They are effective for learning, for the same reason. They take real life people and situations and help you to enter into their thoughts and feelings, so as to understand the issues and think how you would deal with them.

Simulation games take this a step further. You actually *become* a part of the situation, acting out your role as though you were there. Then you step back into your real identity and analyse how you felt, why you responded that way, how others reacted and so on. Out of this experience you can learn a great deal which could help in meeting the real experience, or a similar one.

Role plays and skits

The simplest simulation games are skits and role plays in which two or more people act out roles assigned to them. Often they may be in conflict with each other, or at least reflect different opinions or personalities. There are usually one or two main issues, though there can be more.

After a few minutes' role playing, the participants step back and reflect with the group on how they felt and the issues which came out.

ROLE PLAYS: HOW TO DO IT

Here are some of the basic principles involved in role playing.

l. The purpose is to try and enter into another person's role for a short time. You need to try and think/feel yourself into another situation.

Some will find this difficult, especially older people. Don't force them. On the other hand, you don't have to be a great actor. In fact, good actors may miss the point, because they are so used to taking other roles. They may not actually think about it enough.

2. The issues and roles should be fairly simple, so that they can be entered into quickly, without elaborate preparation. Sometimes brief introductions need to be prepared, giving the person's background etc.

The actual role play should not go on too long. Usually 5 – 15 minutes is enough unless it is more elaborate, like the games in the next section.

3. Reflection on the role play is vital. You must give time for the participants to step back and return to their real selves. Sometimes this can be difficult, if they have got right into their new role! Then the whole group needs to think about what happened, why people behaved as they did and what are the issues and lessons to be learned.

This is a very important time – otherwise the game remains just a game.

There are two more role play games to try out on pages 101–102.

Look back to unit 5, (pages 73–79). Can you find any examples of situations or case studies which could be turned into role plays, with two or more people acting out the different parts?

IDEAS

Here are a few of them…

■ Whose experience is true? (page 73) – the young men in the train
■ The blind men and the elephant could also be a good skit which would amuse everybody and then lead into a serious discussion
■ You could get people to role play the views of people of different faiths, – Hindu, Muslim, Buddhist, secular, Marxist and so on. Somebody else could be a Christian trying to share their faith, perhaps through dialogue and personal witness (page 92 and 93)
■ The church workers and the slum people (page 74) could be acted out
■ The Gandas' situation (page 75) would make an excellent role play
■ '12 Easy Ways to Offend…' could become a series of short skits, and some could be developed into longer role plays (page 76).

You may have seen other possibilities. You could find more in units l–4 as well.

■ **Computer games**
You can get computer simulation games about mission, from simple problem solving to complex situations. The number of these is bound to increase and they will be very useful.

■ **'Experiences'**
You can plan a programme for an evening, or even a weekend, which helps people to 'experience' life in another culture or situation. An 'African evening' or an 'Asian weekend' could include games, quizzes, music, greetings, visual and audio presentations, cooking and eating appropriate food and then reflecting on the whole experience. With imagination and creativity, the effect is powerful.

■ **Activity packs**
On a smaller scale, you can get 'activity packs' with quizzes, worksheets, and other opportunities for active response, often with a cassette tape or pictures to fill in the background.

BIG GAMES

Essential group reading before playing any of these games…

From simple role plays with little preparation we can move on to much more elaborate games designed for groups of 16–60 or even more!

In these games a life situation involving a whole community has been fully described and a large number of roles have been defined, so that a whole group can interact.

The principles are the same, but there are multiple role plays going on and it is much more complex – and more like real life.

You could work out a game like this in your group, or you can get hold of a specially prepared one. Here are two games which are currently available for groups to play…

The Development Game

In the Development Game, everyone takes on the role of an African villager or member of a visiting development team. They act out their role according to the information on the character card they are given, and discuss the village's needs and the development team's suggested action.

The Development Game comes complete with 90 character cards, a slide set with taped commentary, map, posters, instructions and information sheets.

It is suitable for a group of 16–70 people and it takes 1.5–2 hours for the whole game, including time to set the scene and then for reflection. Most of the time is spent in actually playing out the roles.

This game can be a lot of fun, as well as giving insight into what it would be like to live in a village community, or to be involved in trying to help to bring change in such a community.

The real theme of the game is

change – how and why we change or resist change.

It would be good to develop a version for life in a city!

The Options Game

This is a game in which the players participate in making life-determining decisions for themselves and their families.

The game simulates the life expectations of a village somewhere in the less developed part of the world. Each player takes a role consistent with a villager and has to fulfil certain choice options.

At the end of the game, each person will be given the opportunity, if desired, of relating how they felt and why they made their various choices.

Each player is given a role and a certain amount of money – not enough for all the demands they face. So they have to make choices – some are literally a matter of life and death.

Other players take the roles of government officials, health workers, educators,business people and Christian workers who all influence the lives of the villagers and their options.

This is a serious game, designed to make people think – and feel.

The focus is on the *choices* that people have to make.

More than a game

There are several other games like this available, mostly from development agencies. *Monsoon* and *Starpower* are other good ones.

They grip people more than they realise. I have seen a bishop and another senior church leader almost punching each other after playing *Starpower*! They had become so

THE DEVELOPMENT GAME

The Development Game is available from Education Department, Tear Fund, 100 Church Road, Teddington, Middlesex TW11 8QE. It costs £5.00, including postage, in the U.K.

absorbed in their roles and the struggles involved.

Problem-solving games

Less emotional are the kind of games where you have to solve problems, without actually taking on roles. These include working out new languages for Bible translation, planning an evangelistic campaign or trying to resolve practical issues.

Some have been designed as board games, where you go round a board and pick up cards which tell you a problem and ask you to respond.

Two player cards from the Options Game, showing the conflicting demands made upon the players. Other characters in the game include a headteacher, a local church pastor and a state school principal.

CONFIDENTIAL
DO NOT DISCUSS YOUR DECISIONS

You are a farmer. You have two bright children, a boy aged 13 and a girl aged 12.

You suspect that you have malaria – treatment is lengthy and expensive. You need medicine **now**.

Both your son and daughter are ready for high school.

You must have food! How hungry you all seem to be.

Land tax – 4 money units. Needs to be paid today. Interest is 20% per week!

YOU HAVE 20 MONEY UNITS

Cross off your available money units as they are used

CONFIDENTIAL
DO NOT DISCUSS YOUR DECISIONS

You are in charge of the local clinic. You have inadequate supplies of medicine and nowhere near enough beds to service the needs of your community.

Normally patients should be charged 2 money units for a consultation, 3 if they need medicine, 4 for an operation and 5 if the problem is more serious.

Because you have so little medicine you have to control your services so that the most productive members of the community are helped.

Female children are obviously the lowest priority. Wives are also not very highly esteemed. A man can marry someone else if his wife dies, can't he?

You don't have to charge the prices above – charge more if you can get away with it.

THE OPTIONS GAME

The Options Game is produced by Compassion in Australia. They have also published a whole series of similar games. For details contact the Education Department at Tear Fund.

YOUR CHOICE

WORKING ON YOUR OWN?

You will not be able to use a game or role play. But I'm sure that you will be able to find another opportunity to introduce some of these case studies and role plays in your church or fellowship. Try them! They will lead to much more effective and enjoyable learning.

Doing things is better than hearing or reading about them!

Now it's your turn!

Try to find out what is available which you could use in your group. Look at WORM in the Resources Section at the end of the book. It is a catalogue that will amaze you with the wealth of resources available to learn about mission. Look for the Activity Packs in WORM and go from there to find what you want. Several of the kind of games we have described are listed there.

Either or...

For the rest of this unit, you have two choices:

1. If you are working in a group and can get hold of a good game, like

The Development Game, try it out in your group. You will need to plan ahead for this.

2. If this is not practical for your group, or you are working on your own, then take another issue from unit 5 and discuss it. But take one of the case studies or problems there and turn it into a role play. You have already identified possible ones on page 97. The two other role plays suggested on pages 101–102 would be suitable for unit 5 questions 4 and 5 respectively.

Enter into the role plays. You will probably find that your discussion is much more lively as a result!

PART B

Going Further

Use this time to take up another issue from unit 5. Use the same format as in unit 5, Part B.

For registered students

Take one of the issues you have studied on your own or in a group and write out your answers to the main question and any other questions that have arisen in your mind. Use the format already suggested.

This can be in note form, about 300–500 words. Send it to your tutor.

ROLE PLAYING

This section contains two role playing games for you to try in your group.

■ **The Outsiders** explores the difficulties in encountering different cultures
■ **The Evangelistic Programme** simulates the tensions between varying approaches to evangelism.

The Outsiders

Objectives
1. to recognise that different cultures have different ways of doing things
2. to experience the feeling of being a newcomer in another culture

Group size
For a group of eight or more people. The larger the number, the better.

Time required
10– 15 minutes

Instructions
1. Divide into two groups, with at least 4 in each group, preferably more. Send the groups into two corners of the room, or if possible into two separate rooms.

2. Explain to each group separately that they have to behave in a particular way. This is their 'culture'.

   For example: one group could be very noisy and extrovert, touching each other a lot, very active.

   The other group could be very reserved and quiet, avoiding contact with each other as much as possible.

   Or they could have certain characteristic gestures, ways of greeting, secret handshakes etc. The two 'cultures' must be as opposite to each other as possible.

   You can decide beforehand and assign the 'culture' to each group.

3. Give them 2–3 minutes to develop their cultures and begin to behave

with each other according to it.

4. Then send l–2 people from each group into the other group. They have to behave according to their own culture, while the group they are visiting continue to behave and treat them according to their own culture. After a minute or two you can pull them out and send in l–2 more visitors each way.

5. Stop the game and bring the two groups together.

■ Ask the visitors if they could discover the 'culture' of the group.
■ Ask how they felt on entering the other 'culture'. Usually they will have felt strange, an outsider, slightly repelled or puzzled by the others' behaviour, etc. Or they may have tried to adapt to the new culture.
■ Ask for any general reflections.

The main point is quite simple: to experience how it feels to go into a different culture.

The Evangelistic Programme

Objectives
Students will be able to…

■ Recognise sources of inevitable interpersonal conflict demonstrated in a real situation.
■ Identify the need for acceptance and trust building in order to resolve interpersonal conflict.

Group size
3–6 volunteers and a group

Time required
30–60 minutes (depending on the size of the group and how long you continue the role play).

Materials needed
Appropriate role play handouts

Instructions

1. Explain the idea of role playing.

2. Indicate that six people will soon be asked to participate in a role play involving missionaries and summer workers. Read the *scenario* (see box below) to the whole group. Of the six, specify the individuals you want to play certain roles.

3. Separate the groups for the role play. The rest will be observers.

4. Brief the role players as well as the observers.

Role players Distribute the appropriate role sheets. Ask that they not share their roles with the other groups. Prime them to play the *role*, not themselves. Don't be afraid of conflict… keep with the roles. Allow 10–15 mins. to work on their roles.

Observers Prime them for observing conflict. What does it look like? Consider the role players' behaviour:

■ What are its sources?
■ Consider communication, listening, conflicting expectations…
■ What are the overt and internal feelings that accompany conflict?

5. Bring everyone back and begin the role play.

6. Stop the action at the crisis point and debrief using these guidelines:

■ Remind them of what a role play is and that they were set into roles. However, although they were playing roles, the feelings were still theirs.
■ **Participants** How did or are you now feeling? Why? (It may be necessary to remind them of the differences between feelings and thoughts.) Deal with the emotions of the conflict. In your perception, what were the problems?
■ **Observers** How did you feel? Why? What behaviour patterns did you observe and what did they indicate? From your observations, what were the problems?
■ Where was the point of conflict or crisis? How did that arise?

7. Crises will always come. The important thing is how we cope with them. How did the two groups handle crisis? How could you help them to develop mutual respect and understanding?

8. Conclusion. In conflict:
■ We need to understand the others' position in order to comunicate.
■ We need to understand our own position in order to communicate effectively.
■ We need to be mindful of our approach, in order to work through the inevitables of differences.

SCENARIO

Four summer workers have recently arrived in the city of Goya where they will be helping the two missionaries who have been here for eight years. The summer workers have spent the last week recovering from their journey and becoming familiar with the food, the heat, and the city. They have done some sight-seeing and have met some of the local church leaders. Today the summer workers and the missionaries are meeting together to plan for two weeks of tent meetings.

Roles
(to be shown only to the respective role players)

A Summer Worker
(1 or 2 could take this role)

You and your colleague spent last summer in another city in this same country. While there you got to know some of the local people and you discovered that tent meetings are viewed as only entertainment for women and children. You further discovered that you could have an effective ministry by playing your guitar and singing in bars, while oher Christians talked with the patrons about the songs. You hope to persuade the rest of the group to try this type of ministry.

You are to act exactly as though this were a real situation. You may say or do anything you feel will be appropriate to your role.

Role B: Another Summer Worker
(1or 2 could take this role)

You have been nurtured in a strong student Christian union and you have much experience in personal evangelism. You have also participated in a summer evangelism project where you used evangelistic films and skits to present the gospel.

You are to act exactly as though this were a real situation. You may say or do anything you feel will be appropriate to your role.

Role C: The Missionary
(1 or 2)

You have been working in Goya for eight years now. This is your 15th tent campaign and while results haven't been outstanding, you have seen people come to know Christ. You assume that the student workers have never participated in a tent campaign so you realise they may need some persuasion and, of course, some specific instructions. You want each one to have a meaningful role this week.

You should decide which one of the missionaries will lead this planning session.

You are to act exactly as though this were a real situation. You may say or do anything you feel will be appropriate to your role.

Adapted from *Student Training in Mission*, Inter Varsity Christian Fellowship, Madison, 1984. Used by permission.

THE WORLD CHRISTIAN

Unit 7

WANTED!
WORLD CHRISTIANS

CONTENTS

PURPOSE

PART A The purpose of this unit is to help you to discover what it means to be a World Christian and to work out some of the practical implications individually and in your church.

PART B You will plan a programme to help your church or group to become more involved in world mission.

PART A

WANTED: WORLD CHRISTIANS

This is God's world and he has a purpose for it. That summarises a lot of what we have learned so far in this book. In a world of uncertainty and sometimes chaos, that is an important truth to hold on to.

The chosen few?

God has chosen to work out his purpose through his people. In the Old Testament it was Israel, God's servant, the model society, intended to be 'a light to the nations'. In the New Testament the mandate is passed on by Jesus to the church, the people of the upside-down kingdom, the servant community. And so the mandate has come to us. We are part of God's people. Who is going to fulfil it?

The chosen few? Missionaries?

That has always been an answer. In practice it has been a small proportion of God's people who have had a vision for and commitment to God's worldwide purposes. There were times when nobody seemed to have any vision. Even after the Reformation it was nearly 200 years before Protestants recaptured the vision (while the Jesuits and others pioneered across the world).

But there is an obvious danger when we limit the mandate to a minority. At best, they become an elite. Other Christians regard them as special, sometimes put them on a pedestal – and assume that they are the ones to do the work, which lets most of us off. After all, they need a special calling…

At worst, they become a stereotype and caricature. We have seen some of the problems and negative attitudes (unit 2). As a result, many people feel that 'missionaries' are irrelevant today, an embarrassing legacy of the 19th century.

Because of this danger, some argue that we should drop the word 'missionary' from our Christian vocabulary:

What about it?

Look at the quote. What do you think? In the light of the Bible's perspective, who do you think should be involved in fulfilling God's purposes?

"We can safely get rid of the word 'missionary', simply because every disciple of Jesus, by definition, is to be concerned with mission. Disciples of Jesus living in downtown Belfast, for example, have no less an obligation to share the good news than those living in Birmingham, Boston, Bombay or Bangkok."
David Porter, The New Christians, GO magazine, January 1990

It is quite clear from what we have seen of the Bible's teaching that all God's people are called to be part of his servant community, helping to fulfil his purposes for the world. So what do we call them?

You may feel that we should not need any special name. 'Christian' is enough, or 'disciple', because all Christians or disciples should be committed to God's purposes. That is true. But sometimes it is helpful to jog our memories, to remind us of an emphasis we may have lost.

David Porter calls for 'global disciples'. Others speak of 'global Christians', or 'Great Commission Christians'. 'Servants' is a good biblical name to use. 'World Christians' is another suggestion. You will see from the title of this unit (and the book) what our preference is!

What is a World Christian?

Every Christian should be a World Christian, a global disciple, a Great Commission Christian, a servant of God. But what does that mean? In this unit we look at three commitments that characterise the World Christian (and should be the characteristic of every Christian). World Christians are:

■ Committed to God's purpose for his world
■ Committed to God's people who are to carry out his purpose
■ Committed to working out God's purpose in daily life

As we look more closely at these commitments we shall see that there are many different ways in which World Christians carry them out. We may need to keep some of the old titles to describe some of their roles. But you can decide that later on.

Committed to God's purpose for his world

This is a perspective and attitude. It means…

■ to see the whole world as one, belonging to God
■ to make yourself available to God to help fulfil his purpose in the world
■ to recognise your part among God's servant people

John R Mott, one of the leaders of the Student Volunteer Movement at the beginning of this century, spoke of the need for people 'with far-seeing views, with comprehensive plans, with power of initiative, and with victorious faith'.
That is the perspective which we need as World Christians. We gain that perspective as we learn about God's purpose from the Bible, discover the situation of the world today, hear from those who are involved in different kinds of service. And we commit ourselves to God to make our personalities and our gifts available to him. This book is intended to help develop and strengthen that perspective.

Committed to God's people

God deals with us as individuals, each uniquely called and gifted. But his purpose will be fulfilled through his people. As we have seen, the Bible does not polarise the individual and the corporate, as so many do today. They are both dimensions of our human life.

So we each have a specific, individual role in God's purpose. But we are not called to be individualistic or solitary. We are to serve as part of God's people.

However, that can sometimes be our biggest problem, as we will see.

What perspective do I have on God's purpose? How much do I know about it? How do I see the world? Is my life available to God?

WORKING TOGETHER

"The crazy situation we have today with well over 100 foreign missionary societies all actively competing for cash and personnel in the UK, all with their own overheads, staff, glossy magazines and professional display stands. There must be a better way... to serve the church and the world."

Graham Cheesman in FACTS Magazine

We cannot get into a detailed discussion of church structure here. Howard Snyder's books are helpful: The Problem of Wineskins, Marshalls, 1975, The Community of the King, IVP, 1977.

One church, many organisations

We saw that in the New Testament the unit for mission was the local church (unit 4, pages 62–63). Paul founded and worked with local churches. They were partners with him in his ministry. It does not seem to be like that today. We have a variety of other structures and organisations. They are often called 'para-church organisations', because they work alongside churches. Missionary societies fall into this category. There are plenty of them – too many, according to some people.

Look at the quote by Graham Cheesman in the margin. This is how it often seems as we try to cope with the proliferation of societies and agencies. But unfortunately it can be equally depressing, if not worse, when we try to work within the context of our local church.

In some local churches it seems that nobody cares about anybody outside their own four walls. (Some do not care for anything inside either.) They are apathetic and parochial. It seems impossible to find anyone with a broader vision.

Or sometimes the church is already committed to its own programmes and activities. It is too busy to take on anything new.

Working within your local church can sometimes be frustrating. So people turn to others of similar outlook and form their own groups.

Where should our loyalty be? To whom do we relate as we seek to become World Christians and to encourage others? Do we stay only with our local church – and risk frustration? Or do we join a group of like-minded people – and risk being cut off? What do you think? Use the margin to make notes.

Does the New Testament give us any guidelines?

Church and society

While the local church is the basic unit of mission in the New Testament, it is not the only one. The local church at Antioch was prompted by the Holy Spirit to set apart and send the first full-time 'missionaries' – Barnabas, Paul and John Mark (Acts 13.1-4). This was very much an initiative of the local church and Paul always went to them to report on his ministry and maintain fellowship.

But Paul also related to the Jerusalem church and in times of dispute the issues were referred there and discussed in council (Acts 15), or with the apostles and elders (Galatians 2:1,2; Acts 11:30; 18:22; 21:15-18).

Paul also had his own team of workers and colleagues. And he recognised and endorsed the ministry of those who worked with more than one church, pioneering, spreading the gospel, teaching and exhorting, (apostles, prophets, teachers, evangelists, pastors – see Ephesians 4:11; 1 Corinthians 12:28; Acts 8:5; 11:27,28; 15:32; 18:27,28; 21:10). This provided a healthy check to prevent parochialism and error, and a stimulus to provide information and teaching and encouragement.

So the New Testament provides us with models for more than one structure, alongside the basic unit of the local church*.

Playing to our strengths

Look at the material in the opposite margin. Which structure is more effective? We need both. The specialised team is flexible and mobile. It can support and encourage its members. But it does not represent the totality of the church. It can become narrow or even eccentric.

The local church provides the base. It represents all the different aspects of the church. But it cannot do everything on its own. It needs specialised groups to carry out specific tasks.

Look at the two boxes below. Can you add anything to either part, or modify it in any way?

In the light of this, what should be the relationship of the local church and the missionary society?

From your experience of the way they relate at present, can you suggest any changes that need to be made?

So if we are going to be World Christians we have to learn to work it out in the context of our local church, as well as perhaps with other groups, as the situation requires.

We cannot be World Christians all on our own.

TWO STRUCTURES

Ralph Winter identifies two basic structures for mission in the New Testament and in the history of the church:

■ **the local church or denomination** (what he calls a 'modality' structure). This consists of different types of people of all ages, from different backgrounds, with different interests. They are bound together by their location. They demonstrate the church's unity and local structure. They are its basic unit.

■ **the specialised team** (what he calls a 'sodality' structure). This consists of like-minded people, bound together by a voluntary commitment and a common task. This is flexible and mobile. It is good for crossing barriers, and entering new situations. Paul's team is a good example. In the Middle Ages the monasteries and other orders preserved the life and mission of the church when the overall structure was dying or dead. Today's missionary societies are modern examples.

THE LOCAL CHURCH

What the local church should do and can do better than any society...

1. Initial discipleship training
2. Discovering, development and exercise of appropriate spiritual gifts (apostolic church-planting, evangelism, teaching, serving, etc)
3. Objective assessment of potential through long-term contact
4. Decision to proceed or give more training in local church
5. Financial support during theological and practical training
6. Discussion of candidate's suitability with missionary society (much more than giving a reference or recommendation is needed)
7. Commissioning by laying on of hands before departure
8. Realistic financial support based on actual costs overseas
9. Continuing communication of genuine interest and loving concern
10. Caring for the parents of the missionary
11. Provision of housing and other needs of returning missionary
12. Pastoral care and spiritual feeding of missionaries on leave
13. Continuing training in home church during home leave
14. Care of children of missionaries in secondary schooling
15. Generous provision for retired missionaries

THE MISSIONARY SOCIETY

What the missionary society can do that most local churches cannot...

1. Detailed knowledge and experience of any particular field
2. Language teaching facilities
3. Orientation in indigenous culture, customs, society and religions
4. Specific medical advice on prophylaxis and treatment
5. Regular pastoral care of the individual missionary overseas
6. Oversight of the missionary's work on the field
7. Support services like visas, work permits, banking facilities
8. Communication with others on the field and with prayer-partners
9. Regular local prayer fellowship
10. Informed policy discussion and relevant strategy
11. Schooling provision for missionaries' children overseas
12. Acting as middleman with indigenous churches

Taken from: *Pray, Give, Go!* The lists are based on the 1988 Henry Martyn lectures, given by Michael Griffiths at the conference of the Evangelical Missionary Alliance.

JESUS' COMMANDS

LOOK

All that is involved in learning more about the situation in God's world. For practical ideas about getting information, see the Resources Section at the end of the book.

PRAY

Prayer is our most important activity – and often our most neglected. We need all our imagination and creativity – as well as discipline, of course – to enable us to continue praying effectively.

You will find some ideas to help prayer for God's world in the Group Activity pages (pages 116–117).

SEND

Prayer is specifically linked by Jesus with sending. God sends people. But it is in answer to our prayer, so we are also involved. That implies that we are responsible to support and encourage them. So sending includes all that is involved in helping people to serve God.

This includes our giving, but much more. It is the whole process of enabling and caring for people. It also includes the previous functions – continuing to pray for those whom God has sent: continuing to look at their situation and the on-going situation in God's world.

How are people recruited, trained and sent? We shall look at that more closely in unit 8.

GO

When Jesus told his disciples to pray for workers to be sent, they became the first answer to their own prayers. So we can expect that World Christians who are looking, praying and sending will also be among those who go.

We also saw that Jesus was already 'going'. He was already involved in his ministry, which led to deepening and growing involvement in the needs of the world.

INTO ACTION

How did Jesus do it?

Jesus is our model. Both Old and New Testaments. show him as the ideal servant, faithfully carrying out the task given by God.

Many passages in the gospels describe his attitude and practice. A key passage is Matthew 9:35–10:1 Look at it now.

Jesus was deeply involved in his ministry of teaching, preaching and healing (verse 35). As he did this, we are told that he saw the situation of people around him (verse 36).

What result did this have…

- in Jesus' own attitude?

- in his command to his disciples?

Seeing

Seeing is basic. We need to be aware of what is actually happening in the world – both the needs and the opportunities. We also need to see from God's perspective: this is his world and its people are his people, whom he loves and for whom he has a purpose.

This kind of seeing leads to changes in our attitudes. It also leads to action. The most important action is to pray (verse 38). Notice that the prayer is very specific. What is it?

What steps did Jesus take to answer the disciples' prayer in Matthew 10:1 and 10:5?

We pray that God's purpose will be fulfilled in his world. But we have already seen that God has chosen to use his people to work with him in fulfilling his purpose. So Jesus' prayer for God's world automatically leads to sending his disciples. They go out, with exactly the same mandate as Jesus had. Compare Matthew 9:35 with 10:1.

A pattern for involvement

So we have here a fairly complete description of the pattern of involvement for Jesus and his disciples, then and now. We could summarise it in the four commands in the diagram on the next page.

It is a dynamic cycle. One action leads to the next and they are all inter-connected.

Which comes first? 'Look' is not an armchair or library kind of looking. Jesus was *already* involved in his ministry. As he was involved, so he became aware of the situation. We could almost say that 'go' is the basic command, in the sense of becoming involved in serving God wherever we are. As we become involved, we see more, we pray more and we send.

World Christians are part of this dynamic cycle.

Working it out in practice

The first step is to determine that we are going to get involved in this dynamic cycle ourselves. Then we need to look around for other like-minded people within our church or group. It is very likely that something is already being done. However adequate or inadequate this may appear to be, it is always better to try to fit into what is already there than to imagine that we know better than others or that we have to go it alone.

There may be need for change and improvement; we may need to take initiatives; we will certainly need to persevere and be patient. But that is a different matter.

Look at the suggestions in the margin on the opposite page. Not all the activities are appropriate – or necessary – for every group. But they provide a framework which is very similar to the four elements we have identified in Jesus' dynamic cycle.

'Going' is an attitude

'Going' is not some dramatic climax for the special few. It is rather our basic attitude of…

■ **ongoing involvement in service to God where we are, according to our situation, experience and gifts**
■ **obedience and faithfulness in doing whatever tasks are put before us**
■ **openness to look for needs and opportunities and discover what our response to them should be**
■ **availability to God in our present situation and any new situation he may plan for us**

In this sense 'going' is part of our everyday discipleship and service. It is for *all* Christians, not just for those with visas and airline tickets.

PRAY, GIVE, GO!

Pray, Give, Go! is the title of a manual produced by Interaction. (Interaction is a key group. For more details see the Resources Section at the back of the book.) It offers 'suggestions to help Christians consider their commitment to the Great Commission'. It is really a manual for World Christians, helping them to work out their role in the context of their local church. It is full of good ideas.

A basic suggestion in *Pray, Give, Go!* is for each church to have a church missionary committee of 3–8 people. The manual gives detailed suggestions for setting this up. Whether or not your church follows that pattern, the functions suggested by the manual for this group are valuable guidelines for any group of World Christians:

1. Education
2. Prayer
3. Special events
4. Resources and information centre
5. Personnel
6. Finance
7. Long-term planning

Pray, Give, Go! by George Baxter and David Lawrence, Interaction, 10a Dursley Close, Yate, Bristol BS17 4EL

THE DYNAMIC CYCLE

What is involved in each step of the dynamic cycle? Here are the four steps, with some of their practical implications…

GO
➡ ongoing involvement

SEND
➡ enabling
➡ caring
➡ giving

LOOK
➡ education
➡ information
➡ resources
➡ special events

PRAY
➡ individually
➡ in groups
➡ the whole church

And as we continue the cycle, each step leads to deeper involvement and commitment.

WHERE DO WE GO?

23%
of the globe (world A) is ignorant of Christianity, Christ and the gospel.

97%
of all Christians are out of contact with non-Christians.

90%
of all evangelism is directed not at non-Christians but at Christians.

91%
of all foreign missionaries are targeting Christian populations in world C.

95%
of all Christian activity benefits only world C, the Christian world.

99%
of all Christian discussion and writing addresses only Christian interests.

99%
of the Christian world's income is spent on itself alone.

David Barrett

We have said that 'going' means ongoing involvement and availability, rather than crossing the ocean or penetrating the jungle.

But for some it will imply just that. There *will* be those (many?) whom God wants to go physically to cross cultural and other barriers in order to spread the good news of Jesus, inviting people to become part of God's Kingdom and to work with him to fulfil his purposes for the world. The pattern for this was established very early in the Bible, with the example of Abraham back in Genesis 12.

Obedience and availability are simple to understand (though they are the hardest part of 'going'). Knowing where God wants us to go in his world is complex. There are many patterns of 'going' in the world today.

Three Worlds

We are not talking about the 'Third World'! David Barrett divides the globe into three distinct worlds (see Unit 1, page 16, and the box below).

World C is not, according to David Barrett, "the same as 'Christendom', 'the Christian West'…nor does it include North America or Europe in their entirety. Non-Christians or atheists or agnostics in heavily-evangelised countries like the USA or Norway or Britain, for example, fall (on our definition) into World B."

Christians vary in their definitions of 'evangelised', 'reached' or 'unreached' people. But there can be little doubt about the balance, or imbalance, of Christian activity today.

Worlds A and B together make up 67% of the global population.

WORLDS A, B AND C

World B: those who have heard about Christ and the gospel but have not yet made a response

World A: those who have never heard the gospel or heard of Jesus

44%
The evangelised non-Christian world
2357 million

23%
The unevangelised world
1231 million

33%
The Christian world
1796 million

World C: Christians anywhere around the globe

It is not easy to fit countries or peoples into this classification, because each contains a mixture. However some of them can be placed in one or other of these 'worlds' because the majority of their population are in that category.

Our Globe and How to Reach It, David Barrett and Todd Johnson, the AD 2000 series, New Hope, 1990.

But that does not mean that 67% – or even 50% – of Christian activity is directed towards them. On the contrary, most of our activity is concerned with Christians (World C). We are simply not in contact with non-Christians, as the material in the margin shows.

In the light of this analysis, where should we 'go' in God's world today? What should be our priority in trying to find where God wants to send his workers? What do you think?

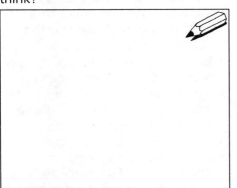

People Groups

Can we analyse the populations of Worlds A and B more closely?

As we have already seen, they do not necessarily correspond to political or geographical divisions, though clearly some regions and countries fall largely into world A or B. In unit 1 (pages 10–11) we thought about 'people groups' – significantly large ethnic or sociological groups of individuals who perceive themselves to have a common affinity for each other. The gospel can spread through such a group without having to cross further cultural barriers.

Because of this, 'people groups' or 'peoples' seem to be one of the most useful ways of looking at the populations of worlds A and B.

For a number of years Ralph Winter and others have been drawing attention to the large number of 'people groups' or 'peoples' which have not yet been evangelised, because they are out of reach of Christian individuals or churches from their own culture.

They have been variously labelled:

- unreached peoples
- unevangelised peoples
- hidden peoples
- frontier peoples

Each description conveys a different shade of meaning and some Christians prefer one to another. But the basic idea is clear: these are 'peoples' among whom there is not yet an indigenous community of believing Christians with adequate numbers and resources to evangelise them.

Somebody will have to cross cultural barriers (maybe also geographical, linguistic and political barriers) in order to give them the opportunity to receive adequately and respond to the good news of Jesus. As we saw in unit 1, it is estimated that several thousand people groups today are 'unreached peoples'.

What does this tell us about our priorities in knowing where God wants us to 'go' in his world?

Look at the *Six Localities* in the margin. This list is not meant to be definitive. Can you think of other types of 'locality' for mission?

It is perhaps implicit, but young people – of different kinds – could be regarded as a separate 'locality' or even several localities. I am not sure how helpful the distinction between 'First' and 'Third' worlds is today, as we saw in unit 1. We could also identify various 'localities' in the Communist world, changing so rapidly. Most of them might fit into the existing list, but would have their own distinctive characteristics. Many parts of the Middle East would also be distinctive.

However, this classification highlights some of the major types of situations. Each is different; each has its particular needs and opportunities. Different people will be better suited to work in different localities.

SIX LOCALITIES

Where do the 'unreached peoples' live? They are not all in jungles or deserts. Maurice Sinclair describes six 'localities' for mission today:

1. Shanty Towns (deprived urban areas in the Third World)

2. Modern sector (privileged city centres or suburbs in the Third World)

3. Inner cities (deprived areas of First World cities, usually situated in an inner ring)

4. Suburbia (privileged areas of First World cities)

5. Third World villages (rural communities in the Third World, often tribal)

6. First World villages (rural communities in the First World)

Ripening Harvest, Gathering Storm, p.160

WAYS OF GOING

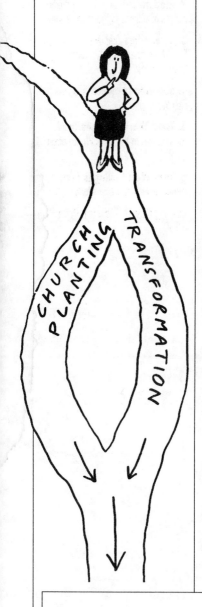

Two approaches?

You may be getting bewildered! It is obvious that different approaches will be needed because of the great cultural, social and religious differences in the world, as we have seen. But is there a more fundamental division?

1. Church planting

Some Christians emphasise the importance of planting churches. The true goal of mission, they say, is to plant churches among all the 'peoples' of the world. 'A church for every people by AD 2000' is a popular slogan. And they feel that too much Christian effort in the name of mission is taken up with other 'good things' – schools, hospitals, development and so on – rather than the real task.

2. Transformation

Others appear to emphasise the need to bring change and 'transformation'. The Kingdom of God means justice for the oppressed and food for the hungry. Only so can its reality be demonstrated, rather than just talked about.

Should we accept these as two different approaches to mission? Is there a conflict, or tension, between them? Should we choose one rather than the other?

A unified approach

It is probably a mistake to see these as two alternative approaches or to prefer either of them. All that we have studied so far, especially the biblical material in units 3 and 4, should lead us to realise that there is only one approach to mission. It is based on the full biblical story, from creation to new creation. Its ultimate goal is the fulfilment of God's purpose for his world and the establishment of his Kingdom.

This begins to take place as people's lives are transformed *and* as they become part of his church. The planting of churches leads in time to further transformation and further church growth.

So we need *one* approach to mission, a wholistic approach that aims at the planting of churches and the transformation of individuals and societies.

But within this overall, unified perspective there are *many* different contributions and tasks, depending on the situation. These range from pioneer evangelism and church planting to working for justice where there are no Christians, from caring for drug addicts to starting schools, from rural community development to radio preaching or tract distribution.

There are also many 'support' activities, like educating the children of Christian workers or 'nurture' activities, like writing devotional books or helping professional Christians to relate their profession to their faith.

All these different tasks must be seen as contributing to the building of the church and the transformation of lives. Where they are not doing so, questions may need to be asked.

But it is important to see our overall task as one, though having many facets.

Can you think of situations where Christians seem to be working in isolation, not contributing to the building of the church? Or where their efforts are too narrowly concentrated on the church? What suggestions do you have?

SIX WAYS OF GOING

To accomplish all these tasks requires not only different skills and spiritual gifts. It also means that there are different ways of 'going' to do them.

Maurice Sinclair identifies at least six ways in which people can be involved in mission (*Ripening Harvest, Gathering Storm*, pp.224–226):

1. Global locals – the largest group: people who are involved in outreach and service in their own 'locality', as well as supporting and encouraging others to go to other 'localities' and situations.

2. Passport missionaries – what are often called 'tentmakers' or 'professionals', people with professional skills which give them a 'passport' to countries and situations where Christian workers may be restricted, or at least full-time cross-cultural witnesses are restricted. *In today's world this is a priority group, needing to be expanded.*

3. Mission partners – the traditional 'missionary' working with churches or from churches, officially recognised by church and government.

4. Veterans – people who have already served in another culture and then move on to a third culture or return to their own culture, but continue to use their skills and experience. These are not necessarily old! Many in their 40s, 30s or even 20s have had such experience.

5. Apprentices – people going for a short period to another culture to contribute and also to learn, so as to be more effective in their own culture or another.

6. Underground witnesses – people living and working in situations where *any* expression of faith is suppressed.

Look at the material in the box above. This list is not complete. Would you like to add to it?

BEING THERE

Here is another list of ways in which people can be involved in mission...

Tentmakers who use their secular employment as a means of mission.

International students using their period of training to get alongside students and also, perhaps, to prepare themselves for further mission responsibilities.

Short-termers lending a hand, but also receiving on-the-spot orientation, again with a view to further involvement in mission at a later date.

Short-term reliefs who enable long-service personnel to take a break.

'It is worth mentioning that the support systems for these various groups may be different. Tent-makers will have a salary; students may have a scholarship; others may have to be fully or partly supported by the gifts of God's people. Yet all are involved in mission, and all need the support of prayer, encouragement and pastoral oversight.'

'Short-termers' and 'short-term reliefs', do not necessarily have to be 'young'! Older people, from professionals in mid-career to retired or twice-retired people, can make extremely valuable contributions, often much more than an inexperienced young person.

From *The End of an Era*, by Dennis Fountain and Jonathan Ingleby, HARVESTER, Paternoster Press, Exeter (reprinted in FACTS magazine, No.23).

SENDING AND SUPPORTING

Not surprisingly, there are as many ways of sending and supporting those who 'go' as you can think of!

Here are some common patterns today:

➡ **Through a missionary society** Still the majority, though that may be changing. Some societies are better than others at maintaining relationships with local churches, both sending and receiving.

➡ **Through specialised societies** Such as…
■ for young people (some begin this way and gradually become middle-aged!)
■ for short-term service
■ for development and relief
■ for Bible translation and distribution
■ for supporting the people or projects of other countries only

➡ **Local churches sending and supporting workers directly** These may be individuals or teams from that church

➡ **Local churches sending short-term teams directly**

➡ **Local churches 'adopting' a people group** This is a recent idea: to link the prayer and concern of local churches with specific people groups. It involves working in co-operation with existing agencies. Look at Part B for more information.

➡ **Individuals or teams going on their own without church links**

➡ **Individuals or teams invited to come by a local church or group in another place**

Probably you can think of other patterns. Which do you think are best?

Important factors

Each pattern has advantages and disadvantages. Two important needs are:

1 **adequate support** and care for the workers, so that they can function effectively and be encouraged through difficulties

2 **realistic direction** of the workers, so that they can work productively and be properly accountable for what they do.

For this reason, individuals and teams going on their own, without church links at either end, are usually an inadequate pattern. Sometimes there is a link at one end but not the other (either sending or receiving). This can also be unhealthy.

Bearing in mind the respective roles of the local church and the missionary society (page 107), it could be argued that a well balanced relationship between local church or fellowship and a sending agency is the most effective pattern for sending and support.

Another important requirement...

...is an authentic partnership between sending and receiving churches. If a church does not yet exist in the place where people are sent, the attitude must still be one that will foster true partnership when the new church is planted.

In units 2 and 5 we thought of partnerships in giving and receiving. So the traffic is not just in one direction but many. Churches may be sending and receiving. They will need to be concerned both for their own local situation and for other parts of the world. They may want help from other churches in other places.

Societies will have to be channels both ways, linking up churches and helping to 'send' and receive the right people for the right place, wherever it may be in God's world.

Today there are many patterns available and possible, by which we can develop rich and effective partnerships between churches, societies and individuals across the world and between cultures. There is nothing more satisfying, especially when the common task is the fulfilment of God's purpose in his world.

Do we need 'missionaries' today? Do we need to keep that word – so loved by some, so disliked by others? What do you think?

My answer to this difficult question is in the margin.

As part of their discipleship some will be required to be available for a specialised ministry (just as some are needed for leadership, or for counselling or teaching). This is the ministry of working in another culture, contributing to the building of the church and the transformation of lives.

What shall we call such people?

MISSIONARIES: YES & NO

■ **No, we do not need 'missionaries.'** We need lifelong disciples – World Christians who are looking, praying, sending and going, in their own place and to other places.

It is a lifelong commitment, not something for two years – or even ten years.

■ **Yes, we do need missionaries.** Because part of the commitment of World Christians is to be available. And there are many different patterns of 'going', as we have seen – within your own culture, in another culture, in another country, long-term, short term or several terms, at different times and different places.

Not everybody can go to another culture. There are qualifications and skills required.

These are not necessarily academic or professional qualifications. Nor do such people have to be young, healthy, single or female, as often assumed! (We shall look further at this in unit 8.)

GROUP ACTIVITY

Note to leader you will need to bring one of your friends' prayer letters for analysis for activity D

A. What are World Christians?

Do you agree with the definition given? (page 105) Do you think this is a helpful name to use? Do you have any other suggestions?

Look at the 'dynamic cycle' (page 109). To what extent are you involved…
■ as individuals?
■ as a group?

B. Local church: doorway or barrier to mission?

How do you evaluate your local church's attitude to mission…

■ in your own locality?
■ in other parts of the world?

How many of the functions listed on page 109 are carried out? Are they done by individuals or by a group?
    What suggestions do you have for your local church?

C. What is the best way to send?

Imagine this local church situation: Christchurch has supported several missionary societies in the past. There is a suggestion in the church committee:

either to stop giving altogether and spend the church's money and time on pressing local needs
or to reduce the number of societies supported in order to take a more personal interest
or to find a new project which the church can concentrate on supporting.

In this connection, some members of the church visited Newtown Church while on holiday. It is situated several hundred miles away in another culture. It was their first exposure to a church in another culture and they are excited. They propose that Christchurch should establish a link with Newtown Church, so that both churches can help each other. They suggest the following:

either sending money to Newtown church (it is poorer than Christchurch)
or sending people to work directly with Newtown Church, supported by Christchurch
or exchanging personnel between both congregations, paying equal amounts
or contacting the missionary society that already works in the area where Newtown Church is
or inviting leaders of Newtown Church to come and discuss what should be done

What advice would you give the Christchurch committee?

D. Prayer for mission

■ How do you pray for mission – as individuals and as a group? What are some of the practical difficulties?
■ Look at the ideas for dealing with prayer letters or other information on the opposite page. Take one of the letters you have received and analyse it as suggested.
Look at the Resources Section for material to help you with prayer.
■ What can we learn from Paul's prayers in Philippians 1:3-11 and Colossians 1:9-12?
Try to pray these prayers for people you know.

E. Receiving and Giving

In what ways can your group receive from churches or groups in another culture or country? Look at the material in the margin.

Can you add to this list? Or make your own list for your situation? Are there other ways in which you have already received from other churches?

Can you suggest ways in which you could receive in the future?

Here are some ways in which the church in Britain (for example) has received from other churches. Have any of them affected your church or group?

■ the Decade of Evangelism (from the African bishops at the Lambeth Conference in 1988)
■ lessons about 'development' and 'transformation' from other parts of the world
■ using new methods for teaching and training people in the churches (like this book!), mostly from South America and India
■ ideas and insights from 'liberation theology'
■ new styles of worship from various places
■ experiences of revival from East Africa and other places
■ evangelists and teachers from other countries, to work with the local people as well as with immigrants

WHAT DO YOU DO WITH MISSIONARY PRAYER LETTERS?

I read it.
Good! But you won't remember much of it.

I stick it up on our missionary noticeboard.
Great! But very few people will read it.

I file it!
Tidy… But filing cabinets don't pray.

So how can I make better use of prayer letters?

IDEA

Analyse prayer letters for the notice board into easily read and assimilated sections. For example…

Bill + Jean in Overthere Land	
Family News	
Activities	
Future Events	
Special	
Praise	

These ideas for prayer letters are taken from *There's a Big World Out There* by Val and Dan Connolly.

GOING FURTHER

STAGES IN YOUR PLAN

1. Before you write anything down or discuss things with others, talk to the leader(s) of your church. Show them this assignment and ask for their suggestions and advice.

There may be things going on which you are not aware of, or ideas and hopes which others have. Or practical difficulties which you had not thought of.

2. Then prepare your draft plan.

3. Again show it to your leader(s) and any others you wish to. Get their further reactions and suggestions. Ask them how the plan can best be implemented. You may be able to agree on the next steps together.

You will probably find it best to look at unit 8 before you finalise your plan. It should give you some helpful ideas on how to involve people through action-based learning.

4. Finally you are ready to make your plan!
Because you will have discussed it twice already with others, you should be able to introduce it and get something started.

FOR REGISTERED STUDENTS

Prepare your plan and send it to your tutor (2–3 pages of A4, we suggest). Include a report on your discussions with church leaders and others and the steps you hope to take.

A. Plan of action

How can your group or your church become World Christians? Prepare a plan of action for your local church. It should include:

■ The present situation: how far are you involved in the 'dynamic cycle' of activities (page 109)? Who is doing what?
■ Steps that could be taken over the next 2 years/1 year/6 months/3 months
■ Resources that you could use, from the Resources Section (pages 137–138) or from elsewhere
■ People to be involved from the leadership of your church, or others.

Look carefully through the Resources Section. Take particular note of InterAction, which is intended to help churches to do exactly what you are trying. You will find their manual *Pray, Give, Go!* extremely valuable. You may also find that there is a conference or other programme that would be relevant.

And don't forget WORM (in the Resources Section)! You will be amazed at how many resources are included there.

B. Read

Ripening Harvest, Gathering Storm, chapters 5 and 6 on different patterns for mission today.

C. Adopt-A-People?

We have already noted (units 1,2,7) the fact that the world can be divided into 'people groups'. Thousands of them are considered 'unreached' today. (There are different figures, based on different ways of calculation).

The idea of 'Adopt-A-People' is that local churches 'adopt' a specific group. They begin to focus their prayer on that group. They also give to support work being done or planned for that group. They may also seek to send workers to that people group, in consultation with other churches or agencies already working or planning to work there. Such consultation is vital: there is no point in trying to re-invent the wheel or bypass those with experience of cross-cultural ministry.

The goal is to see that a viable church is established among the people of that group.

What do you think about this idea?

An obvious advantage is that it gives a clear focus and goal for a local church.

On the other hand this approach calls for co-operation and careful co-ordination to make sure that efforts are not wasted or duplicated. It would be a mistake to assume that our church could necessarily do better than missionary societies or other churches that are nearer to that people group.

But such co-operation and co-ordination is surely possible with today's resources and technology? That's certainly true, but could also be part of our problem. Is technology the basis for our mission? Or just a very useful resource?

But this idea is too important to be ignored. For full details write for the information pack *Missing Faces in the World Church*, available from: Evangelical Missionary Alliance, Whitefield House, 186 Kennington Park Road, London SE11 4BT.

CULTURE ₀CULTURE

THE WORLD CHRISTIAN

Unit 8

BEGINNING NOW

CONTENTS

PURPOSE

PART A The purpose of this unit is to help you to look at different ways of preparing to be a World Christian. You will identify qualities needed for work in another culture and the essential ingredients for effective training, by looking at four case studies.

PART B You will suggest ways to develop effective learning projects in your church or group.

THE ESSENTIAL QUALITIES

Becoming a World Christian doesn't happen overnight.

By now you will have realised that there is a lot to learn. There are…

■ issues to think through and biblical *understanding* to gain
■ *attitudes* to develop
■ *skills* to acquire

What do you think are the most important qualities needed? Look at the list on the opposite page. Are there others you want to add? Write them below.

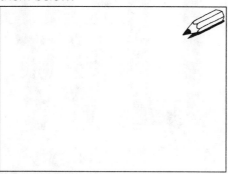

Attitudes

A group of mission leaders were discussing this question. They agreed that the most important qualities are *attitudes*:

■ our commitment to God and his purposes
■ how to relate to others with love and humility
■ how to understand and accept ourselves, with all our positive and negative features

This is because serving God – in any capacity – means relating to other people of all backgrounds. This is especially true when we work in another culture. And the biggest problems in any kind of service arise out of our attitudes.

Another group of mission leaders were discussing, in the late Fifties, what kind of missionaries were needed in the new post-colonial era. Several spoke of technical skills and professional qualifications. Then an elderly Indian stood up and said 'My country needs saints'.

'Saints' in the Bible are those who belong to God and as a result are *different* in their attitudes and behaviour. They are those who are growing in their relationship to God and commitment to his purposes.

Skills and understanding

After attitudes come skills and understanding…

■ how to understand people of other cultural and religious backgrounds – how to communicate the gospel in a way that is relevant to them
■ how to equip and enable others and serve as a catalyst
■ how to develop an appropriate lifestyle and manage time and other resources, especially in another culture
■ how to think biblically and creatively
■ how to reflect and learn from all that is going on around you in daily life
■ how to grow in understanding of our own faith and practise it in daily life

Getting ready

It takes time to develop these qualities. But that doesn't mean that we can't do anything now. On the contrary, if we want to be World Christians it's important to begin now.

There are many ways to prepare ourselves. For all of us, it begins with our basic discipleship, growing closer to Christ, prayer, God's word, fellowship, worship and service in our local church…

As we do this we begin the dynamic cycle that we looked at in Unit 7 (page 109). We will be able to see more, pray more, and discover new ways of loving and serving God.

If we use even a part of the resources listed in the Resources Section (pages 137–138) it will take us a long way.

The fact is that most of us already have access to all the resources we need to become World Christians.

Other options

What about more specialised preparation? What about Bible College?

There are many different ways to receive more specialised preparation, if that is what we need. They include:

■ full-time residential study
■ part-time courses
■ learning on the job; working with a church or organisation
■ short-term exposure to other cultures: two weeks to two years…
■ distance learning courses
■ sandwich courses

You can probably add to this list. Write your suggestions below.

Three essential ingredients

Each has its own strengths and limitations. We each need to find out what is most appropriate for us, because everybody is different and has different needs. We cannot say that one approach is the best, or can replace others. Any of the ways above could be right for us. Probably a combination would be best, since it would give different strengths and compensate for any limitations.

We cannot try to assess these different types of training here. But we will highlight three essential ingredients that are important in any effective preparation for World Christians (in other words, for all Christians):

■ Preparation should cover all three areas we have looked at – *attitudes*, *skills* and *understanding* – not just one or two
■ preparation should be based on 'learning by doing'
■ preparation should include 'learning in context'

What do these things mean? We are going to look at four case studies and try to see how they illustrate these three ingredients.

WHAT MAKES A CROSS-CULTURAL WORKER?

What are the qualities to look for in someone thinking of work in another culture? Against each item below fill in whether you think it is Vital (V), Helpful (H) or Not important (N)…

☐ good at languages
☐ healthy
☐ adaptable
☐ eats anything
☐ has the strong support of the home church
☐ under 30
☐ has received Bible and missionary training
☐ single
☐ called by God
☐ has been ordained
☐ already active as a Christian in their own culture
☐ going with a missionary society
☐ has been to university
☐ has a sense of humour
☐ guaranteed financial support
☐ good at preaching
☐ can stand loneliness if necessary

Discuss your choices. Can you think of any biblical support for your reasons?

How would you provide training to develop the qualities which you think are important?

This list is taken from *There's a Big World Out There*.

1. TOO YOUNG FOR MISSION?

This material is by **Steve Chalke**, National Director of Oasis Trust.

Spiritual apathy?

As I travel round the country, a strange thing happens. They take you on one side just before you speak and say, 'Steve, you've got to understand the problem here… it's the spiritual apathy, especially amongst the young people. We just can't get them involved…'

The truth is that young people are not apathetic. I have never met an apathetic young person in my life. Teenagers have endless energy, enthusiasm, drive, commitment. The problem is that it is often not harnessed or driven in the right direction. It has been diverted into areas that have nothing to do with their Christian faith. So they appear apathetic and lifeless; but the enthusiasm and energy *are* there.

How do we tap that energy? How do we present to young people the challenge of mission involvement; of being World Christians; of taking up their cross and following Christ in a way that they can relate to and understand and respond to?

If you look at young people around the world, you discover this: *They* are the ones who get involved. There was a lad in our youth group who was against experiments on animals. Every Saturday he stood in the High street campaigning. It could be raining, snowing, anything, he would be out there, doing his bit.

Young people are single-minded. They see things in black and white. They know what's right and what's wrong. They want to give their lives for something that is worth it. They want to believe in something. In the Middle East, when terrorists drove lorries packed with explosives into American embassies, it was teenagers that manned the lorries. It's teenagers who are out on the streets of Belfast.

➡ For further details about **Christmas Cracker**, turn to page 132…

Who are teenagers?

Teenagers, or adolescents, are those who are *in between*. Adolescence is leaving the harbour of childhood and setting out on a dangerous voyage, across uncharted waters, to the land of adult life. In childhood all your decisions are made for you and all your needs are taken care of.

Now, as teenagers, they've left behind the security of childhood and are heading for adult life, without yet its privileges. They are stranded somewhere in between. They are looking for challenge and responsibility. They want to *do* things, to try out their abilities. But they are not always given the chance. They're in between.

Why Christmas Cracker?

Mother Teresa said , 'You can't change the world by giving your money. You've got to dig deeper than your pockets. You've got to give your time and your energy.'

We want young people to get involved in mission, by giving their time and energy. That's exactly what young people want to do. They don't want just to hear, they want to get involved as well.

The old Chinese saying is very much to the point:'I hear and I forget, I see and I remember, I do and I learn'. Plato taught that thinking should precede action. Karl Marx teaches that action and thought must go together.

All our churches have been based on the philosophy of think first and then do it. Being a Christian is all about what I think about. Practical involvement, say in outreach, comes as an optional afterthought. But Jesus called men from 'catching sprats', as he might have put it, straight into catching real men.

In Luke 6:10, Jesus calls the 12

disciples. In Luke 9:1, less than three chapters later, he sends them out two by two. When they come back to Jesus, filled with a sense of inadequacy, he could have reacted in a negative way, expressing regret at having sent them out.

That's what many of us do:

'We can't send young people, because what will they say about us? Our image could really suffer'. Our image couldn't suffer any more than it's already suffering with a lot of young people.

Jesus, by contrast, shows them what they should have done. Then in chapter 10, just one chapter later, after they've blundered, he sends them out again, on their own, in his name. Not just 12, but 72. You don't have to be that good at maths to work out the relationship of 12 to 72 and the training role that the 12 must have played in sending out the 72.

When I trained for the ministry I spent four years training and then I was just a wet-behind-the-ears beginner. Jesus calls a group of fishermen and others, and in three years they're out on the road without him. But not even three years; in a matter of months they're out training others.

We need to harness the energy of young people. Not just to get them giving, but to get them involved in something really meaty that they're excited about. Remember, they're yearning for responsibility. The rest of society shouts them down. It's a tragedy if the church does it as well.

Getting started

The above article is based on Steve Chalke's address to the annual conference of the Evangelical Missionary Alliance, November 1990.

Read the article. You will be excited at what he describes.

What are the most important lessons that you learn from this?

Two important things to grasp are...

■ You don't have to wait to be involved in mission and God's service. You can begin *now* by doing what you can, where you are. The younger the better, because young people want responsibility and grow by it.

■ You learn by doing. Action and thought go together.

Is this just an insight which Karl Marx had?

Steve Chalke shows that this was in fact Jesus' approach to training. See also how Anton Baumohl describes it in the margin material. This is 'learning by doing', apprenticeship on the job.

Paul used a similar approach. Look at Part B if you want to study this further.

This approach is not just for young people! But perhaps young people are more willing to make mistakes or take risks? That is an important element in 'learning by doing'.

2. SHORT-TERM = SHORT-LIVED?

Short-term service projects are increasingly popular.

Time to Give

Time to Give, published by the Christian Service Centre, is an amazingly useful directory, listing 'Opportunities for Short Term Christian Service.' It lists well over 40 opportunities for all ages, in Britain and almost anywhere else in the world. Everything from STEP to PEP, Agape to Crusoe, SPOT to Street Invaders!

A lot has been written about the advantages and disadvantages of this kind of service, especially in another culture. Some argue for the flexibility and economy, or the freshness of approach which new people can bring. Others point out the lack of experience, the problems of adaptation and continuity. Some question the commitment of short-term workers.

Most of these comments look at short-term projects from the perspective of *service.* But is that the only way – or the best way – to look at them? Most people agree that what you *receive* and *learn* in a short-term project is more important than what you *give.*

ON TRACK

Look at this list of objectives for a short-term programme. Put (S) beside those that emphasise service and (T) beside those that emphasise training and learning. Some may include both.

(This programme has a variety of 'tracks' of different lengths, for people of different backgrounds, ages and interests).

1. To stimulate an interest in cross-cultural Christian service and a commitment to world mission.

2. To introduce Christians to the cultural background, human needs and Christian community of another culture, with a view to developing an understanding and appreciation of the people of that culture.

3. To provide an experience which will make global disciples, helping participants grow in faith, increase in maturity and assess their involvement in world mission.

4. To facilitate the long-term recruitment of appropriately qualified and trained Partners to serve as God leads.

5. To develop the support base in sending countries through enthusiastic, envisioned, informed and committed participants who will communicate their experience and support Partners through their prayers, friendship and finance.

6 To contribute by providing skilled and professional short-term assistance to meet specific needs or openings.

A test case

Look at the boxed material, describing the aims and objectives of *On Track,* a short-term programme. All of the aims above seem to emphasise training, learning and personal growth, except the last objective, which applies to certain projects with skilled personnel.

But how will the participants learn? They are not joining the programme to sit in a classroom or read books! What do you think?

This is another example of 'learning by doing'. They will be doing things, observing others, making mistakes, asking questions, reflecting on their experience.

This will also be 'learning in context' as they will be in a new situation, perhaps in another culture. That alone can be a significant learning experience. All of us can remember the first time away from home, in a new job or in a new culture. It raises all kinds of new questions and opens us to new ideas and perspectives.

Avoiding negative experiences

Sometimes our experience may be negative. People experience 'culture shock' – when they find the local people cold and apparently unfriendly (as in Britain),when they face a new climate (cold or hot), experience high technology and urban pressures, or extreme poverty or disease. They can come away confused, bewildered, even disillusioned.

How can we make sure that short-term projects really are learning and training experiences? What do you think should be done to help people to learn and grow?

Before, during, after...

You have probably given several suggestions. We have to work at this at every phase of a short-term project.

■ **Before** It is important to help people realise that their primary purpose is to learn and grow through their experiences. They will have a contribution to make. That should not be under-estimated. But it is exactly as they try to 'do their bit', with its limitations as well as achievements, that they will learn from their successes and even more from their failures.

■ **During** Time needs to be allowed for study and reflection. There should be a person on the spot who supervises and guides the participants and can spend time with them to talk and pray over what they are experiencing. Some projects have a study programme built in, which is extremely valuable.

■ **After** 'De-briefing' is important, both at the project and when people get back to the place they were sent from. It is also very valuable to have a further period of reflection a few weeks or months later, when people have had time to settle back and think more about their experience.

Which areas of learning do you think will be most affected by short-term projects with this kind of training built in? Attitudes, skills or understanding?

Every project is different – and every individual is different – so it is impossible to give an overall answer. But it is likely that most people would learn in all three areas. They would certainly learn in the area of attitudes.

So short-term service – whatever its other advantages and disadvantages – can be an extremely valuable way of preparation and training to be a World Christian.

3. CHANGING THE STRUCTURES?

In unit 7 we thought about the role of the local church in sending people into God's service. But when they go to serve in another culture, with churches of that culture, should not those churches also have a share in their selection and training?

Graham Cheesman asks:

> "But who trains the missionaries? With the situation today including very respectable seminaries, in many cases part of the training could well be done within the country of service and under the direction of the church there – an agreed package of training between the sending and receiving churches."

> But who chooses the person to go? We should be working towards a joint choice of the candidates with input from the local churches that send and input from the churches that receive."

FACTS Magazine No 28, p8

A radical proposal

Look at Yemi Lepido's proposal in the box opposite. What value does this proposal have for *training* and *preparation*?

What other values does it have?

Do you see any limitations or difficulties?

This is a very exciting proposal, because it emphasises 'learning in context'. People will learn in the new situation into which they are going. As we have already seen, they will have all kinds of new questions and experiences. So their learning will not just be theoretical, but will affect their attitudes and skills as well. They will be able to work with colleagues of the new culture and learn from their way of working.

It will be valuable in other ways, especially because it emphasises genuine two-way partnership (look back to our discussion of this in unit 5 question 5, pages 88–89).

But of course it will be difficult to implement because, as the writer himself points out later on, people's attitudes take a long time to change, especially with regard to money...

But there are already examples of people getting this kind of training in the culture in which they are hoping to work – Swedish, German, Japanese and Koreans studying in India; Koreans and Brazilians in Britain; Swiss in China; Americans in Egypt and many more. Do you know of other examples? How valuable have they been?

CHANGING THE EXISTING STRUCTURE OF WESTERN MISSIONARY SOCIETIES

The suggestion I am about to outline assumes a church planting organisation similar to those already existing in the UK. Let us call it the United Missionary Society – UK.

(a) UMS – UK develops a link with a similar organisation in Uganda of similar status and acceptance in the Anglican Church in Uganda as in the Church of England.

(b) Missionary training centres are set up in the UK and Uganda. A joint training curriculum is worked out, based on the needs of the church in the UK and Uganda, to prepare British missionary partners for service in Uganda and Ugandan missionary partners for service in the UK. A basic missionary orientation course will be received in the home country after acceptance as missionaries; a 'settling-in' or language orientation course will be undergone on arrival overseas; and a debriefing orientation on return for home leave.

(c) A British selection panel travels to Uganda to interview recommended candidates and submits a list of approved candidates to the Uganda Board. Similarly a Uganda selection panel travels to the UK on the same exercise. The final placement of approved mission partners in UK or Uganda is made by the respective Home Boards. Such an

arrangement 'will greatly enhance the incarnational life-style, the missionary will feel truly recruited by the partner church and the latter will feel truly the employer' (Revd. Canon Simon Chiwanga).

(d) A mutually agreed length of service is worked out (two years or longer with so many weeks of local leave and home leave).

(e) Each Home Board pays the air-fare of its mission partners. The receiving Home Board (ie UMS-UK for Ugandan partners) determines salary scale and pays the agreed sum. While on home leave the Ugandan mission partners will receive a Ugandan salary scale (not the UK scale).

People have asked: 'Is it realistic to expect the Ugandan church to pay local salaries to missionaries?' My answer is an emphatic 'yes', if the Ugandan church is really serious about replacing missionaries with equally qualified Ugandan Christians.

Some say, 'By all means do so for the African missionary in the UK' – presumably because they think that Christian workers in the UK receive a living wage. In actual fact, the average salary for a Christian worker would not be sufficient for the African missionary in Britain if he chose to live on an African diet; send his children to private schools;

fulfil his extended family obligations; provide hospitality for streams of visitors, and so on. Having worked in London for five years, it is true to say I was financially better off in Nigeria than in the UK. Not only could I buy more for less currency in Nigeria, but workers of registered charitable organisations enjoy income tax exemption!

This arrangement will in future allow African missionaries to be sent to different parts of the world because their living expenses will be paid by the receiving church or local agency.

From *The Cost of Reciprocal Partnership in World Mission* (An African Perspective), BCMS Crosslinks, August 1989.

4. CULTURE TO CULTURE?

You are already part of *Culture to Culture*! This book is the first part of a new training course, complementing all that is already available.

Who is it for?

It could be for anybody! It is for World Christians. But it is *specifically* intended for…

■ 'tentmakers' preparing for witness through their professions
■ short-term workers, before or after their term of service
■ mission catalysts and representatives in local churches

What's special about it?

Culture to Culture has at least five main features…

It is an open learning course, designed to be as accessible and flexible as possible. People will be able to study at the time and place which suits them (using distance learning material). They can do the whole course or parts of it. They will also be able to use the resources of different institutions and perhaps transfer credit.

It is integrated, combining different types of learning experience. These include:
■ theoretical study through distance learning materials
■ practical experience of life in another culture
■ interaction with a personal tutor and group
■ attending a summer school
■ ongoing involvement in their local church and ministry

It enables participants to remain involved in their local church and ministry. In fact this is part of their training. They can also continue studying the course as they begin their cross-cultural ministry.

It is complementary to all the types of training we have been looking at. It could be used along with short-term projects, or 'on the job' training, or in conjunction with other types of training. A person

CULTURE ᵗᵒCULTURE

The seven modules are as follows…

Introduction
1. The World Christian – An introduction to mission for individual study and for groups in local churches.

Practical experience, guided reflection and reading
2. Issues in Mission Today – An introductory study of some of the pressing issues in cross-cultural mission.

3. Entering Another's World – How to understand people of another culture and another faith.

4. Personal Ministry in Mission – How to understand your role and gifts for mission, explored within the local church.

Group meetings with personal tutor
5. Personal Development – Understanding and developing our attitudes and personalities, within a small group.

Distance learning with correspondence tutor
6. Understanding the Bible – How to understand the Bible in its culture and apply it to another.

7. Theology in Context – Learning how to 'do theology' in ways appropriate to a new cultural setting.

You can choose the modules you wish to do and combine them in different sequences.

Further details: CULTURE to CULTURE, St John's Extension Studies, Bramcote, Nottingham NG9 3DS. (Telephone: 0602 251117). Use the application form at the end of this book.

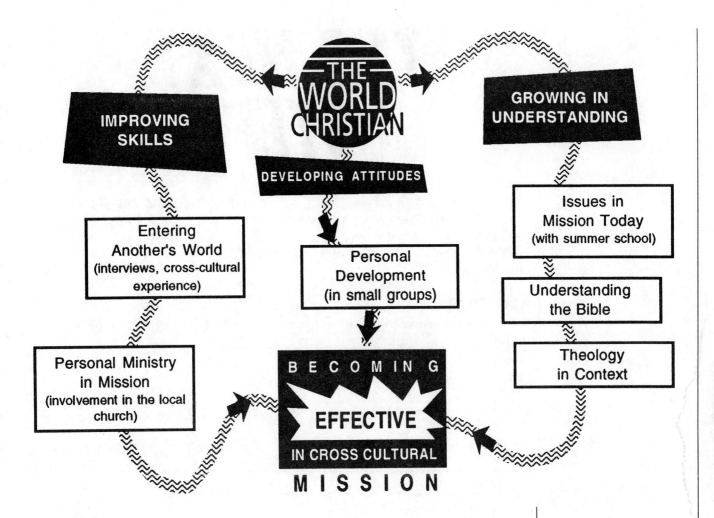

THE WORLD CHRISTIAN

IMPROVING SKILLS

DEVELOPING ATTITUDES

GROWING IN UNDERSTANDING

Entering Another's World
(interviews, cross-cultural experience)

Personal Development
(in small groups)

Issues in Mission Today
(with summer school)

Understanding the Bible

Theology in Context

Personal Ministry in Mission
(involvement in the local church)

B E C O M I N G

EFFECTIVE

IN CROSS CULTURAL

M I S S I O N

could begin the course in their own culture and continue after reaching another culture.

It aims at growth and learning in all three areas that we have thought about – attitudes, skills and understanding. It consists of 7 distinct modules. Each module combines understanding, skills and attitudes in different ways. But they are also grouped into three main paths, as you can see from the diagram. You can choose the modules you wish to do and take them in different sequences.

How long is the course?

The whole course is equivalent to one year's full-time study, but will normally be spread over 2–3 years. We hope to add a second stage based on participants' experience of at least two years of cross-cultural ministry. It will include a wide range of topics and will reflect their own backgrounds.

The course can be used by those preparing for cross-cultural ministry and by those who have already begun.

THE NEXT STEP

How do we begin? That's really up to each one of us. God wants us all to be World Christians. There is no lack of opportunities to become involved in serving him right where we are. And as we do that we enter the dynamic cycle which Jesus himself practised and passed on to his disciples, with great urgency.

Reflection

Spend some time looking back over your study. What have you found most useful?

What has been less useful?

What are some of the main things that you have learned?

How much was completely new to you?

What are the topics or issues that you would like to pursue further? How will you do it? Do you know of available resources?

Action

What action are you going to take (or are already taking) in response to what you have learned?

Write down at least three specific things that you plan to do, and when. They may be immediate, or things that you will do over the coming months. You do not have to share these with anybody else. But writing them down will help you to focus your thinking and remind you of what you have planned! Write them in the margin.

The material on CSC is by **Paul Lindsay**. For further information on the Christian Service Centre write to CSC, Holloway Street West, Lower Gornal, Dudley, West Midlands DY3 2DZ.

What is the Christian Service Centre?

You may still have questions and uncertainties about where you fit in. The Christian Service Centre is the best place to start looking. Try their questionnaire.

If you tick 'yes' for any of these questions, that's one reason why the Christian Service Centre exists.

CSC was founded to provide an independent advisory or consultancy agency for evangelical Christians, helping them move forwards into God's place and plan of service for them. Enabling the different shaped pegs to fit!

CSC provides a source of information on different aspects and avenues of service; on organisations and ministries that are already on the move; on opportunities and openings needing filling; on materials to instruct, inform and help.

CSC provides a service to Christians needing help in their search. A network of experienced advisors throughout the UK voluntarily give of their time to meet with and help people determined to find their place in God's work. Special conferences are held which are designed to help people understand themselves and their place in service.

CSC also provides a service to Christian organisations with opportunities for more workers. By registering such vacancies with CSC, it provides an ideal platform for matching such needs with some of those CSC seeks to advise and direct.

CSC is a stimulant raising the needs that touch God's heart and provide a chance for people to serve this world.

CHRISTIAN SERVICE CENTRE QUESTIONNAIRE

Are you/do you...   **Yes   No   Don't Know**

- Thinking seriously about Christian service?
- Want to know where you fit into God's plan?
- Considering a 'tentmaking' experience abroad?
- Want help in understanding your gifts?
- Want to know what opportunities there are for working abroad?
- Interested in short-term service opportunities?
- Want to know who does what in Christian work?
- Wondering how and where to prepare for service?
- Want to know where your gifts can be best used?
- Wish there was someone of experience to talk these things through with?

CHRISTMAS CRACKER

The power of teenagers

Teenage power is worth harnessing. Witness the remarkable success of the Christmas Cracker project. In the weeks leading up to Christmas for the past two years more than 30,000 teenagers joined forces to help the world's poor. In an innovative national fundraising project they converted more than 200 vacant high street premises, church halls and offices into temporary Eat Less – Pay More restaurants.

The combination of support from parents and friends (and the microwave) made it possible to serve home-cooked meals in simple surroundings. For the three weeks that the restaurants were open they tried anything to raise money – they auctioned glasses of water, borrowed circus bears and danced in the streets.

In addition they organised nearly 500 special Cracker Day events in schools. They worked hard and had great fun. All of the proceeds were channelled through relief and development agencies to projects in the developing world. In the total of about six weeks that the restaurants were open, nearly £1,000,000 was raised.

How it started

The project was organised by the

Christmas Chracker charity, based on a concept and very successful pilot scheme in 1983. The impetus came when the originator of that project made his first visit to India and saw the appalling conditions first hand. By the time he arrived back in England he had concocted a plan to repeat the fundraising restaurant idea on a national scale.

There was extensive planning and preparation. A ten-week course taught young people about poverty, development and Jesus' attitude to the poor. Then came the tremendous logistical campaign to turn the theory into substance. At the end of the trading period many of the teenagers were asking 'what's next?'

Curiously, raising money was not the primary goal of the exercise. As national director of the Cracker project, Steve Chalke, explains:

"We aim to show young people that their action can make a difference. The problems of the world are so great that it is hard to act. We want to cultivate a positive and energetic attitude to sevice that will outlast any particular project."

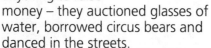

IN 1989/90, CHRISTMAS CRACKER...

- Mobilised thousands of young people around the country
- Helped organise 230 restuarants and 480 special events
- Generated a wave of interest in the developing world
- Obtained extensive media coverage including BBC Newsround, BBC National News, TV AM, Sky TV, BBC Radios 1 and 4, BSB, Channel 4, *The Times*, *The Independent*, *The Daily Telegraph*, *Mail on Sunday*
- Stimulated extensive coverage on local radio, TV and in the regional press
- Sent 15 young people to India for hands-on experience
- Launched Cracker projects in Europe, Africa and Australia
- Twice entered the Guinness Book of World Records — for pulling the World's largest Christmas Cracker (120 feet) and signing of the World's largest cheque (16.8 metres)
- Gave the public an opportunity to respond to the needs of the third world in a context that was conducive to real discussion
- Joined forces with BBC Radio 1 to launch the Breakfast Show appeal, *Water for India*. A national collection of 64 million postage stamps raised over £12,000 for the provision of clean water to drought-stricken areas of India
- Provided young people with practical business experience
- Raised £1 million for overseas aid and development

Give them a bigger Peace

GROUP ACTIVITY

A. The essential qualities

Look at the list of qualities for people working in another culture (page 121).

Discuss the choices you made there. Can you give any biblical or practical reasons for them?

How would you recognise a person in your group or church with the potential for working in another culture?

Should your group be actively looking for such people? Or do you wait for people to volunteer?

B. The best way to learn is...

The four case studies (pages 122–129) illustrate different ways of preparing for mission. They all include the three essential ingredients mentioned on page 120 – attitudes, skills and understanding.

Has anybody in the group had experience of any of these ways of preparation? For example...

■ involvement in an 'action' project like Christmas Cracker (or many others like it)
■ short-term service in another place
■ any kind of internship or practical experience placement

Share your experiences. Did you feel that all those ingredients were included in your experience?

C. Culture to Culture

Culture to Culture is a training course that tries to take advantage of different ways of preparation and to complement other types of programmes as well.

Has anybody in the group had any experience of this type of training? Share your experiences and ideas.

D. Widening the Circle

How are you going to share what you have learned with others in your church or fellowship? Look at the suggestions in Going Further, section B (page 134).

What could you do as a group?

What about ordering some of the material in the Resources Section for your group, especially catalogues like WORM or manuals like *Pray, Give, Go!*?

E. Evaluation

Spend some time in your group looking over the eight sessions.

Share your responses to the questions on page 130.

What action are you going to take, as individuals or as a group?

Close your session by praying for each other.

■ thank God for what you have learned together
■ thank God for what he is doing in his world
■ ask for God's guidance for the next step for each member of the group
■ pray for wisdom and strength for each of you to know God's will and to do it

GOING FURTHER

A. Passing it on

One of the best ways to reinforce your own learning is to pass on what you have learned to others. You will learn the most from doing that, whatever the effects on the others!

So use this time to think through how you can do this.

■ If you have studied this book on your own, then an obvious step would be to get a group to work through it. You would be well placed to lead such a group, or you could get somebody else to lead it and contribute to the group yourself.
■ Another way is to use material suggested in the Resources Section, especially from a catalogue like WORM or a manual like *Pray, Give, Go!*
■ Or you might use one of the Bible study outlines suggested there, or another one that you know. They are in general shorter than *The World Christian*, because they do not necessarily require individual study in preparation for a group meeting. You could lead a group through one of them. *There's a Big World Out There* would be a good choice.

But perhaps the best way would be to apply the principles we have looked at in this unit. How would you…

■ help people to grow in attitudes as well as skills and understanding?
■ help people to 'learn by doing'?
■ help people to 'learn in context'?

Is your church or group already involved in some kind of 'action' project? Does it allow enough time for reflection and learning, as well as 'doing'?

If you already have such a programme, can you suggest ways to make it more effective for *training* and *preparation* to become more effective in God's service?

If you do not, can you think of ways to develop a suitable programme? Perhaps this could be part of the plan that you have been working on in unit 7 (page 118).

'Learning by doing' is very powerful, as we have seen. Try it out!

Spend some time looking through the Resources Section and thinking about which ones you could use, to help you develop the most effective approach to preparation.

B. Reflection and response

How did you find the material in this book? If you can send a copy of your reflections (page 130–131) it will be very useful for evaluation and improvement. You do not need to include your personal plans for action, if you do not want to.

Send to: *The World Christian*, St John's Extension Studies, Bramcote, Nottingham NG9 3DS.

Thank you!

FOR REGISTERED STUDENTS

Please send a copy of your reflections to *your tutor*, not to St John's.

JESUS AND TRAINING

It is important to learn from Jesus' approach to training his disciples. In Part A we identified three elements in Jesus' training. Remind yourself of them (page 123). Look up the following passages. Beside each one write the elements of training which are mentioned there.

For example, look at Mark 3.14–15. The 12 disciples were to be with Jesus. This would give them opportunities for *observation* of his life, miracles, etc. They would also receive *explanation* from him.

Jesus also sent them out for preaching and casting out demons. This was their *involvement* in practical work.

Write your notes on the other passages:

☐ Mark 4:34

☐ Mark 4:39–41

☐ Mark 5:37

☐ Mark 6:7

As we continue through the gospel we find this process repeated again and again. Mark 6:30–31 introduces a new development. We could call it a second phase of training.

The disciples come back to report on their involvement, the assignment given by Jesus in Mark 6:7–9. Jesus takes them with him for a time of reflection on what has happened. From this will come new lessons for their future involvement.

So the process of training is a cycle, in which *involvement* is followed by *reflection*, which prepares for further more effective *involvement*.

We can illustrate this learning cycle as follows:

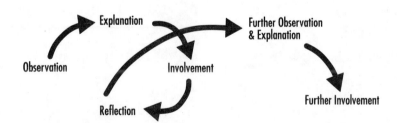

In Mark 6 the reflection process was interrupted by the crowd. Jesus used this as a further opportunity for teaching the people (6:33–34) and then for training his disciples (35–37). How do you explain Jesus' command to the disciples in verse 37? What element of training was this?

Jesus seems to have been testing his disciples, giving them involvement, but this time in an assignment that was clearly beyond them. They did not know how to solve the problem, as the other gospels make clear. Then Jesus gave a further demonstration of his power by feeding the crowd. This would have meant so much more to the disciples because of their own unsuccessful attempt to deal with the problem.

So the cycle could include the disciple's *failure* or inability, as with the crowd:

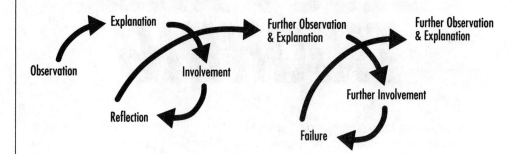

Sometimes the cycle would be started from a *question* of the disciples or a *situation* which they observed, perhaps puzzling or remarkable:

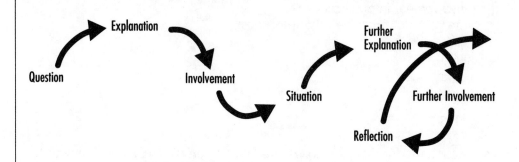

Look at the following passages and indicate whether the training cycle included a *failure, question* or *situation* observed (sometimes more than one). Briefly summarise Jesus' further explanation or example to be observed:

- ☐ Mark 8:14–21
- ☐ Mark 9:18–19, 25, 28–29
- ☐ Mark 9:33–37
- ☐ Mark 9:38–41
- ☐ Mark 10:10–12
- ☐ Mark 10:13–16
- ☐ Mark 10:23–25
- ☐ Mark 10:41–45
- ☐ Mark 11:20–23
- ☐ Mark 12:41–44
- ☐ Luke 10:17–20
- ☐ Luke 22:24–27

This training cycle enables us to learn from our experiences in ministry, both successes and failures. (Notice how much the disciples' failure is highlighted in the gospels. Jesus gave them the freedom to fail – one of the most difficult and yet important things to allow in the training process).

It also helps us to see that training is an ongoing process, which all of us need and in which we can help each other. The fact that Jesus gave so much attention to training his disciples reminds us of its importance.

RESOURCES SECTION

This is not exhaustive – just a few key resources for World Christians.
   Please note…

1. Each resource listed will lead you to further resources.
2. Details are given here of resources in the UK. If you live or work in another country or region you will need to look for the appropriate equivalents there.

Bible study
(Group or individual)
There's a Big World Out There
Val and Dan Connolly: The Vicarage, 87, Perseus Place, Purbrook, Portsmouth PO7 8AW
Clearly written, cleverly illustrated: excellent material for groups, which does not assume any prior knowledge. Not just Bible study but a complete introduction to widen horizons.

Bible Study Outlines on Mission
Interserve Scotland, 12 Elm Avenue, Lenzie, Glasgow G14 9PX
Another simple and thought-provoking series of studies on key passages.

Dirty Hands: 'What the Bible Says…'
Dirty Hands, P.O.Box 115, Dudley, West Midlands, DY3 2AN
Six concise studies; part of the Dirty Hands Guide to Action.

Longer study courses
Culture to Culture
St John's Extension Studies, Bramcote, Nottingham NG9 3DS
The open learning course in mission.

Perspectives on the World Christian Movement: A Reader
Ralph Winter and Steven Hawthorne (eds): William Carey Library, available from the US Center for World Mission, 1605 Elizabeth Street,

Pasadena, CA 91104, USA
A compendium of 85 extremely valuable articles on biblical, historical, strategic and cultural aspects of the world Christian movement. Almost a study course in itself.

World Mission. An Analysis of the World Christian Movement
Jonathan Lewis (ed):
1. The Biblical/Historical Foundation
2. The Strategic Dimension
3. Cross Cultural Considerations
William Carey Library, available as above
A three-volume series which includes key articles from the 'Perspectives' Reader and other sources and provides a study guide.

Opportunities for Christian Training
Christian Service Training Council, 4, Woodbank Close, Wistaston, Crewe CW2 6SD
A comprehensive directory of training courses of all kinds – residential, part-time study, distance learning, correspondence courses, group study.

A Small Directory of Non-Residential Courses
TEEF, available from Rev Mike Butterworth, Oak Hill Theological College, 6 Farm Lane, Southgate, London N14 4PS (£1.75 post free)
Lists non-residential courses on the Bible or Christian ministry available in the UK.

Books and magazines
There are too many books to list here. You will find a few in the introduction at the front of the book, and many, many more listed in WORM (see below).

FACTS Magazine
Glenburn House, Glenburn Road South, Dunmurry, Belfast BT17 9JP
Published three times a year. Each issue brings together key articles from

different sources on a particular topic. Extremely valuable.

Pray, Give, Go!
InterAction,10a Dursley Close, Yate, Bristol BS17 4EL
A manual with everything you need to get your church or group involved in mission. Detailed guidelines and practical suggestions.

3rd Track
Tear Fund, 100 Church Road, Teddington, Middlesex, TW11 8QE
Material for youth leaders. Strong graphics, lots of lively ideas for active programmes.

Lookout
EMA, Whitefield House, 186 Kennington Park Road, London SE11 4BT
A comic-style magazine for 7–11 year olds, creating awareness of God's work in our world. Full of puzzles, cartoons, stories and activities.

Material for prayer
World Prayer News
Lancing Tabernacle, 20 Abbotts Way, Lancing, West Sussex BN15 9DH
Detailed guidelines for prayer, divided into continental regions. Published six times a year under the auspices of the EMA. Annual subscription: £1.85 including postage.

Operation World
Patrick Johnstone (ed), STL / WEC, 1986.
A guide for prayer, with valuable information about the needs of the world. Every country is listed, with detailed material on its general situation and the situation of the church.

Directory of resources
WORM (World Outreach Resource Material)
EMA,Whitefield House, 186 Kennington Park Road, London SE11 4BT
An amazing compendium of (almost) all the resources available for teaching and learning about mission: videos, books, activity packs, filmstrips, films, tapes, slides, posters, OHP transparencies, drama, games – and lots more...! If you use even a tenth of what is listed here you will be extremely well informed...

It's updated every year, so get the latest edition.

Information about opportunities, guidance
Christian Service Centre
Holloway Street West, Lower Gornal, Dudley, W Midlands DY3 2DZ
The Centre provides information on opportunities for service through its literature, conferences, personal enquiries, stalls at conventions and a network of advisors who can be consulted around the country. It is a valuable service and the natural first place to enquire about anything connected with ways to serve.

Pickenham Resource Centre
The Pickenham Trust, North Pickenham, Swaffham, Norfolk PE37 8LG
Information about job vacancies all over the world and advice and orientation for people thinking of taking up such jobs.

Time to Give
Opportunities for Short-Term Christian Service. Christian Service Centre (address above)
Over 40 opportunities for short-term service in the UK and overseas. Guidelines on how to choose and even a centralised application form (like UCCA!).

Key organisations
Evangelical Missionary Alliance
Whitefield House, 186 Kennington Park Road, London SE11 4BT
The EMA brings together organisations and individuals involved in world mission, for fellowship, co-operation and sharing of ideas and resources.

Interaction
10a Dursley Close, Yate, Bristol BS17 4EL
InterAction works with churches to encourage them in world mission through conferences, literature and providing information and ideas. It is a ministry of the EMA and the Evangelical Alliance.

RECOMMENDED READING

There are lots of good books on mission. Here are a few basic books that you can read alongside this one:

Essential resource books

Ripening Harvest: Gathering Storm, Maurice Sinclair, MARC/STL/CMS/EMA, 1988 (£3.95). This is an excellent introduction: biblical themes, historical background, world Christianity and the missionary task. If you register for credit, you will be required to read parts of this book.

God's Mission: Healing the Nations, David Burnett, MARC/EMA/STL, 1986 (£2.75). The biblical story of mission, very practically related to key issues today.

The Quiet Revolution, Robin Keeley (ed.), Lion Publishing, 1989 (£7.95). First published under the title *Christianity: A World Faith*, 1985. Still available under that title. A fascinating survey of worldwide Christianity.

Mission and the Crisis of Western Culture, Lesslie Newbigin, Handsel Press, 1989 (£1.25). An essential introduction to the urgent task of mission in secular cultures.

Prepared to Serve, Tear Fund/Scripture Union, 1989 (£3.95). Practical suggestions for living and working in another culture.

Operation World, Patrick Johnstone (ed.), STL/WEC, 1986. A guide for prayer, with valuable information about the needs of the world. Every country is listed, with detailed material on its general situation and the situation of the church.

The World Christian Starter Kit, Glenn Myers, WEC/STL 1986 (£1.50). Pocket-sized, astonishingly comprehensive survey of what God is doing in the world and what still remains to be done. Very good value.

ANCC Booklets on Mission. A new series of short studies by experts on key topics. The first in the series is: *What's so Unique about Jesus?*, Chris Wright, Monarch, 1990 (£2.50).

Clash of Worlds, David Burnett, MARC, 1990 (£8.99). A fascinating study of the different ways in which people look at the world—our 'world-view'.

For reference only ...
The World Christian Encyclopedia, David Barrett (ed.) OUP, 1982. Encyclopedic and exhaustive, but compelling reading. If you can borrow it for even an hour, you will be richly rewarded.

Videos

If you can use a video in your group, it could provide a useful supplement to the written material, especially in Units 1, 5 and 7. Here is a list of the 'Top Ten' recommended by the EMA:

Talking Guidance, Talking Mission (29 mins, SIM International). How can you know God's will for your life? Personal guidance experiences from a pastor, an SIM candidate secretary and a mission researcher.

Through Closed Doors (32 mins, AWM). Arab World Ministries are involved in strategic missions in the heart of Islam worldwide. Discover the challenges and opportunities of their work in this unique documentary.

Across Cultures (25 mins, INTERSERVE). Discover how you can be a global Christian, working in partnership with believers from other races to speak God's truth into different cultures.

Catching the Tide (23 mins + 15 mins, INTERSERVE). The stories of four Asian people who against all the odds became Christians. Also, Asian Christians and white churches—can they really mix? Should they?

On Wings and Water (37 mins, UFM Worldwide). The story of how the gospel is changing the lives of some of the 750 tribes in Papua New Guinea.

The Price That's Paid (33 mins, Wycliffe). A video quiz which explores how much blood, sweat, tears and laughter are poured into the translation of the Bible into new languages.

Caught in Time (25 mins, Leprosy Mission). This compelling documentary, shot in Nepal, contrasts the tragedy of late diagnosis of leprosy with the triumphs possible through modern care methods.

Listeners in the Field (28 mins, FEBA). The story of FEBA Radio in Mozambique and their part in bringing hope and practical aid to a people battered by war.

Rivers of Gold (40 mins, UFM Worldwide). God is at work in Brazil. This excellent video captures the excitement of life in a country where the church is expanding rapidly.

The Race (14 mins, SIM International). A concise look at how SIM has and is seeking to 'run the race marked out' (Hebrews 12:1) right around the world.

(This list of videos is taken from *Tell the Nations*, EMA/Elm House, November 1990.)

Also ...
Jesus Commands us to Go (7 mins, SIM International). A vivid picture of the church around the world and our joint responsibility for mission.

If you plan to use a video you will need to make arrangements to get hold of it well in advance!

Games

In Unit 6 you will have an opportunity to try out some of the simulation games available today. If you plan to do so, you will need to get hold of one in advance. Look at Unit 6 now for details.

REGISTERING FOR CREDIT?

Please fill in the form below. We will put you in touch with your correspondence tutor as soon as possible.

I want to study **The World Christian** for credit with a tutor. Please register my name.

Name
Address
Postcode   Telephone

I enclose a cheque for £25.00 to cover the cost of tuition. Send with your remittance to:
St John's Extension Studies, Bramcote, Nottingham NG9 3DS (Tel: 0602 251117).

Please use the space below to tell us about yourself: something about your background and why you are interested in doing this course. It will be useful to your tutor to have this information.

MORE INFORMATION ABOUT CULTURE TO CULTURE?

Tick the box below if you would like more information about the rest of this course.
(See Unit 8 for details)

Name
Address
Postcode   Telephone
Church Affiliation

☐ Please send me the prospectus for **Culture to Culture**.
Send to: *St John's Extension Studies, Bramcote, Nottingham NG9 3DS*